The Balkans

A Captivating Guide to the History of the Balkan Peninsula, Starting from Classical Antiquity through the Middle Ages to the Modern Period

Free Bonus from Captivating History
(Available for a Limited time)

Hi History Lovers!

Now you have a chance to join our exclusive history list so you can get your first history ebook for free as well as discounts and a potential to get more history books for free! Simply visit the link below to join.

Captivatinghistory.com/ebook

Also, make sure to follow us on Facebook, Twitter and Youtube by searching for Captivating History.

Contents

Introduction: What Are the Balkans?

Before we even begin to look at the history of the Balkans, it is pertinent to address the basic definition of what the Balkans are in the first place. You may have heard the phrase "Balkanized" and wondered if there was a connection. There is. The term arose in the aftermath of World War One when the Allied powers were faced with the daunting task of sorting out the divisions that had erupted in the Balkan Peninsula in southeastern Europe.

The Balkan Peninsula is ringed by the Balkan Mountains in the north, the Adriatic Sea in the west, the Black Sea in the east, and the Ionian and Aegean Seas in the south. The Balkan region was often used in the 19th century to describe the sections of southeastern Europe that had at one point been part of the Ottoman Empire. It was the end result of centuries of struggles between the Christian kingdoms of southeastern Europe and the Islamic armies that had pushed through Asia Minor.

The Ottoman Turks—from which Asia Minor itself would become known as "Turkey"—had once established a base in the region. Although Islam was the prominent religion in the Ottoman Empire, the Ottoman rule was more or less tolerant of other religions. We must say more or less because even though it was not Ottoman policy to forcibly convert Christians to Islam outright, there was constant pressure on the people of the Balkans to do so.

Muslim tradition allowed Christians to maintain their faith as long as they accepted a second-class citizen status known as the *dhimmi* and agreed to pay a hefty tax. Having said that, the incentives to convert to Islam were great. By becoming a Muslim, the average person of the Balkans would gain more rights and would be free from paying the annual *dhimmi* tax known as jizya. Those wishing to be free of the routine discrimination that was brought about due to their faith made the decision to convert to Islam.

Nevertheless, some who held dear to their faith refused these enticements and remained Christians. One must keep in mind that although Christians were second-class citizens, the Ottomans were more tolerant than many Christian kingdoms of that day and age. All one has to do is look at Christian Spain toward the end of the Reconquista, when Spanish Muslims were basically given the choice to convert to Christianity, be expelled, or be burned at the stake.

So, as hard as life was for a Christian under Islamic rule, the Ottomans did show at least some form of tolerance. However, the tolerance that Muslims extended toward Christianity and Judaism in the Balkans was not extended to other religions for the most part, although this changed over time. The Quran states that Jews and Christians are fellow "People of the Book," and as such, they were accorded some level of tolerance. If you happened to be of any other faith, all bets were off.

At any rate, the greater degree of tolerance that traditional Muslims showed toward Christians, in particular, resulted in certain parts of the Balkans becoming fairly evenly split between Muslims and Christians. A large portion of residents struggled under these hardships, and some caved in to the pressure and converted to Islam. Sadly, as these differences of faith became more pronounced as time passed, they would become a source of much agitation and hostility between the two sects.

The more divisive things became, the more "Balkanized" the region became. As of this writing, eleven countries comprise the Balkans: Slovenia, Serbia, Romania, Macedonia, Montenegro, Moldova, Kosovo, Croatia, Bulgaria, Bosnia and Herzegovina, and Albania. It is worth noting that even though Greece is in the Balkan Peninsula, Greece is generally not considered a Balkan state. Its northern neighbors of Albania and Macedonia most certainly are.

Now that you know what the Balkans are as a geographical and cultural region, it is time to jump into its history. We hope you enjoy your journey of the history of the Balkans, from its very beginnings to its most recent events.

Chapter 1 – Balkan Beginnings

"Historically, the Balkans have been an incubator of war."

-Pat Buchanan

Long before anyone knew what to call the region we now refer to as the Balkans, there was a long history of human settlements. According to the archaeological record, humans have lived in the Balkans as far back as fifty thousand years ago. This puts the first Balkan settlers squarely in the Paleolithic period. Artifacts indicate that these first settlers consisted of small, transitory tribes, which followed the animals they hunted and gathered whatever wild-growing crops they could as they moved.

Shortly after the end of the Last Ice Age, around 10,000 BCE, these hunter-gatherers began to put down more sturdy roots. From 10,000 BCE onward, there is evidence of regular habitation along the Danube in places like modern-day Romania and Serbia. These settlements boasted a wide range of pottery and other trappings of a more sedentary lifestyle.

Around 7000 BCE, we find the remains of major agricultural operations, which are indicative of permanent farms in the region. Traces of bean, wheat, pea, and barley farms have been discovered that date back to this period. There was also an explosion in the use of cooking utensils and religious artifacts, and there is evidence that the domestication of animals was widespread.

One of the oddest archaeological finds is several human figurines with fish-like mouths and other strange features. These figurines could have been a part of religious practice or even just tools for some good old-fashioned story-telling around the campfire. Since there was no written record at this point in human history, we can only guess what their actual purpose might have been.

These prehistoric residents tended to build their villages on the same piece of land over and over. Archaeologists refer to these ruins of layered human habitation as "tells." A gigantic, multi-layered tell can be found in the modern-day Bulgarian city of Karanovo. It is stacked some forty feet high, and it is believed that it was steadily occupied for well over two thousand years.

One interesting aspect of these early settlements, considering all of the wars and bloodshed that would erupt in the Balkans later on, is the fact that none of these early habitations indicate any attempt to establish defensive bulwarks. The settlements were set up completely undefended, right in the middle of a floodplain. This indicates that at this point in history, large-scale invasions were not common in the region. As long as they banded together in small groups, these prehistoric Balkanites could fend off the occasional troublemaker and did not fear the prospect of a huge army of outsiders swooping down on top of them.

For a time, the Balkan settlers were allowed to progress their society in relative peace, and eventually, a more complex society began to emerge. These advances were evident in the more complex pottery that began to appear, which indicates the advent of specialized craftsmen. There is evidence that, at this point, these settlers began to take on specialized roles within their society. And around 5000 BCE, the first copper- and gold-crafted objects began to emerge in the region of modern-day Bulgaria. The prehistoric people of the Balkans crafted rings, bracelets, and necklaces with these minerals.

So far, everything was going well for the ancient denizens of the Balkans. Fast forward to 4000 BCE, however, and something happened to these peaceful settlers. Many sites were suddenly depopulated at this time. There is no explanation for this sudden departure, but it has been heavily speculated that organized warfare had finally reached the Balkans. It is possible that bloody fighting made refugees of these early Balkan residents.

It took a few centuries, but the Balkan civilization finally began to revive around 3500 BCE. Archaeologists have found evidence of large-scale agricultural communities being established around this time. In the coastal regions, new innovations began to take shape, and for the first time, the locals began to grow what would become a staple in the region—grapes and olives. Soon, staple trade goods, such as wine and olive oil, would be common fare.

And apparently, the settlers had learned from the past. These settlers were no longer building villages out in the open. Instead, they were strategically placing them on more easily defendable terrain, such as on top of hills or situated around other natural barriers. This was an obvious effort to keep would-be aggressors at bay.

Around this period, an influx of migrants from the eastern steppes began to emerge. These newcomers brought horses and oxen with them, which became more prevalent throughout the Balkan region. Archaeologists have detected a much more stratified society during this time period, in which clear social strata were developed with a much greater emphasis on organized defense. And just as military prowess was taking precedent, there appears to have been widespread honoring of the veterans of conflicts.

During this period, all throughout the Balkan region, one could find graves that were apparently dedicated to warriors. They were given a special distinction, as their gravesites are unique from other sites. These highly honored fighters were buried with their weapons by their sides, and they seem to have been held in great reverence.

Around the year 2000 BCE, the Balkans began to leave their prehistory behind. Instead, we find the peoples of the Balkans influenced by the Mycenean civilization, which stretched from Crete and into most of Greece. The Minoans left their imprint through elaborate stone palaces, exquisite pottery, and stunning frescoes. The Mycenean civilization ended abruptly in 1200 BCE, although no one is exactly sure why this happened.

The Greeks began to excel in the southern reaches of the Balkan Peninsula shortly after the Mycenean civilization's demise. Although the Greeks' ancestral memory of the Myceneans was rather vague, they tended to view themselves as inheritors of the Mycenean civilization. The Greeks, of course, would go on to flourish, establishing great cities like Athens, Attica, Sparta, and the like. Rather than having a centralized kingdom such as the Myceneans did, the Greeks were content to have their own independent city-states.

Even so, their influence managed to reach from the Mediterranean all the way to the interior of the Balkans. But the Balkan people in the interior were also heavily influenced by the tribes of people who came from even farther north, from regions such as modern-day Transylvania and Carpathia. These fierce warrior tribes of the north introduced deadly steel weapons to settlers in the Balkan interior.

The Iron Age spanned roughly from 1200 BCE to 600 BCE, and the Balkan interior was heavily influenced by it. In fact, by the time a certain kingdom began to rise up in Macedonia, just north of Greece proper, the Macedonian warriors would be much better equipped and organized for war. This would prove crucial when a man named Philip II rose up to become king of Macedonia in 359 BCE.

Philip would rally a large, unified Macedonian force that would march on Greece itself. The hopelessly divided city-states of Greece didn't stand a chance against this Macedonian onslaught. And soon, all of the Greek city-states became clients of Macedon. However, King Philip would be assassinated in 336 BCE. This opened the door for his son, Alexander, to succeed him.

Alexander, better known as Alexander the Great, would go on to forge a huge empire that spanned the entire Mediterranean and included most of the Balkan Peninsula. Alexander not only conquered but also spread the virtues of Hellenism everywhere he went. Greece was known by the locals as the Helles, so Greek culture, therefore, was called Hellenism.

Alexander the Great may not have been a Hellene by birth. Nevertheless, he was a huge supporter of Hellenism, and he made sure that the Balkans were heavily influenced by it. Shortly into his reign, in 335 BCE, previously loyal vassals in the Balkan interior began to revolt and tested the young king. Alexander embarked on a military campaign in the Balkans, in which his forces easily subdued and pacified the agitators, which allowed him to consolidate his Balkan territories.

Once he had the Balkan interior in his back pocket, Alexander the Great went on to wage war with the Persian Empire. Beyond all odds, he managed to strike a great blow to the mighty Persians. He deposed their king and annexed much of the old Persian Empire into his own dominion. From this point on, the Balkans were part of a vast empire that stretched through Greece, Asia Minor, Persia, back through the Levant, and into Egypt.

However, after Alexander's abrupt death in 323 BCE, his mighty empire quickly split into several factions, as Alexander's generals took over various portions of his territory. Shortly after the demise of Alexander and his unified empire, a group of Balkan people known as the Illyrians began to come to prominence. The Illyrians lived just north of Macedonia in what comprises modern-day Albania and parts of Bosnia and Dalmatia.

Today, the modern nation of Albania has tried to reconnect with its Illyrian past, suggesting that an unbroken chain of descent between the ancient Illyrians and modern-day Albanians still exists. If so, it would make the Albanians the elder statesmen of the Balkans. At any rate, by the time of the Roman Republic's eastward expansion in the late 3rd century BCE, the Romans and the Illyrians became intense rivals.

The Illyrians were an increasingly frustrating thorn in the Roman Republic's side because of their habit of allowing privateers (a fancy word for pirates) to ambush Roman ships crossing the Adriatic Sea. Things came to a head in 230 BCE when the Romans sent a group of diplomats to speak with the leader of the Illyrians—Queen Teuta—ostensibly to resolve the matter peacefully. The meeting did not go too well.

According to Greek chronicler Polybius, the Roman diplomats "began to speak of the outrages committed against them. Teuta, during the whole interview, listened to them in a most arrogant and overbearing manner, and when they had finished speaking, she said she would see to it that Rome suffered no public wrong from Illyria, but that, as for private wrongs, it was contrary to the custom of the Illyrian kings to hinder their subjects from winning booty from the sea."

Queen Teuta was basically telling the Romans that she had no control over her subjects and that if they wished to attack Roman shipping, there was not a thing that she could do about it. Incensed, the Roman diplomats attempted to enlighten the queen on Roman law and how Rome made it a point to punish their own citizens for any "private wrong" that they may have committed.

Polybius tells us one of the Roman diplomats immediately barked back with angry sarcasm. "Oh, Teuta, the Romans have an admirable custom which is to punish publicly the doers of private wrongs and publicly come to the help of the wronged. Be sure that we will try, God willing, by might and main and right soon, to force thee to mend the custom toward the Illyrians of their kings."

Although the diplomat did not say it outright, he was clearly suggesting that if Queen Teuta could not control her own subjects, then perhaps, "God willing," the Romans would conquer Illyria and make the queen subject to Rome so that she would have to enforce Roman law and finally put a stop to all of those pesky pirates.

Queen Teuta seethed with rage at being spoken to in such a manner. Polybius writes that she just couldn't let it go. So, when the envoy was returning to their ships to disembark, she sent a group of warriors to attack them.

After the survivors of this ambush returned to Rome to inform the Senate of what had happened, the Romans launched an all-out war against the Illyrians. The war would drag on for decades, and Illyria would not come under complete Roman control until 167 BCE. It is said that once the Roman conquest of Illyria proper was complete, the refugees fanned out to the Herzegovinian mountains, where future settlements in the more remote regions of the Balkans would be established.

They could run, but they could not necessarily hide. In the ensuing years, as the Roman Republic transformed into the Roman Empire, the Balkan Peninsula in its entirety would fall into Rome's grasp.

Chapter 2 – The Balkans and the Romans

"Remember all those references to Macedonia as the oasis of peace in the Balkans. You only really appreciate it when you have lost it."

-Boris Trajkovski

The region now widely known as the Balkans has always been the crossroads of various world powers. The Romans, Greeks, and Persians had all claimed pieces of the Balkan puzzle at one time or another since the very beginning of recorded history. In these early days, however, it was the Romans who eventually won out. By the 1st century CE, virtually the entire Balkan Peninsula was under the control of the early Roman Empire.

Well-known Balkan cities, such as Belgrade, Sofia, and Ljubljana, were all founded by the Romans. They were known by different names back then, of course. Belgrade was Singidunum, Sofia was Serdica, and Ljubljana was Emona. All of these Balkan cities have deep Roman roots.

It has been said that during the classical days of Rome, the people in the Balkans entered one of the most peaceful periods of the region's history. During the Pax Romana, those who resided in the

Balkan Peninsula could count on Roman security, Roman roads, Roman laws, and a robust Roman-based economy.

Although Hellenism was encouraged, the Romans displayed tolerance, for the most part, for local customs and traditions. And the Romans certainly left their own mark. For instance, Romania was named after them. The small Balkan country of Croatia is renowned for sporting the ruins of one of Roman Emperor Diocletian's royal palaces. The site can be found in the Croatian town of Split.

For Diocletian, this Croatian mansion must have been akin to a country resort where he could get away from the burdens of Rome for a while and just relax. Interestingly enough, Croatia, in more modern times, is getting back to its resort town roots, with many parts of the country becoming popular tourist destinations due to its easy access to the Mediterranean and a generally pleasant climate.

And, of course, Albania, the seat of the former kingdom of the Illyrians, became an established part of the Roman fold. This is evidenced by the massive Roman road called Via Egnatia or, as it translates, the "Egnatian Way," which stretches from Albania all the way to Constantinople (modern-day Istanbul). It was along this vast stretch of road that the armies of Julius Caesar and his rival, General Pompey, would wage war against each other in 48 BCE. Illyria would certainly become the crossroads of an empire.

In fact, in the stomping grounds of Illyria (modern-day Croatia, to be exact), Roman Emperor Diocletian was born in 242 CE. Diocletian was indeed at home in the Balkans, and it was mentioned that he kept a palace in the region. Although Constantine the Great is often credited with moving the focus of the Roman Empire east, in truth, the process had already begun by the time of Roman Emperor Diocletian.

In Diocletian's day, the Balkans were much more stable than the western front of the Roman Empire, which already had to deal with repeated skirmishes with the wild tribes of northwestern Europe. During his reign, Diocletian realized that the Roman Empire was becoming too unwieldy to deal with, so he created a system of co-emperors. He ended up assigning a reliable officer of the Roman armed forces named Maximian as the emperor in the West, while he remained sovereign from his seat in the Balkans in the East.

Despite the eastern portion of the empire being more secure than the western frontier, there was still plenty of opportunities for conflict to erupt. During Diocletian's reign, in 285 CE, the Roman emperor found himself having to raise a force to do battle in the Balkans due to a rebellious group of locals known as the Sarmatians. Diocletian tried his best to put down the revolt, but this highly mobile group was able to avoid complete defeat by simply relocating to territory out of his reach. It would not be long before they would cause trouble for the Romans once again.

Diocletian's protégé, Constantine the Great, would eventually rise up as the sole Roman authority in 324 CE, and he, too, hailed from the Balkans. Constantine was born in modern-day Serbia. And likewise, Constantine would make the Balkans his permanent home base after forging the new eastern capital of the empire, Constantinople, in 330 CE. Located on a thin strip of land known as the Bosporus Strait, which connects the terminus of southeastern Europe to Asia Minor, this strategic foothold would rule the Eastern Roman Empire and thereby the Balkans for over one thousand years.

Part of Constantinople's success was due to its massive Theodosian Walls, which were erected by Emperor Theodosius II in the 5th century, although they were rebuilt as time passed. By this time, the western half of the Roman Empire had fallen, and all that remained was the eastern half of the empire with its Balkan base. In time, some attempts to regain lost ground would be made. But for the most part, the Eastern Romans or, as they would come to be known, the Byzantines would begin to be more and more on the defensive rather than the offensive.

Chapter 3 – The Balkans and the Byzantines

"The people of the Balkans are like a dysfunctional family. We may fight and argue, but in the end we are family."

-Vlade Divac

In 527 CE, at the start of Byzantine Emperor Justinian's reign, Constantinople—the capital of the Byzantine Empire—was the largest, most advanced city in Europe. Constantinople had eclipsed the fallen city of Rome, and while western Europe was entering into its "Dark Ages," Constantinople and its surrounding Balkan territory remained wealthy and well-connected. During this period, early Byzantine monuments and architecture began to crop up in the region. Most notably, the Church of Holy Wisdom, better known as the Hagia Sophia, was constructed in Constantinople. The church, which is now under the control of Turkey, still stands as a marvel of Byzantine architecture.

As strong as Byzantine buildings were, the true glue that held this empire together was its successful blend of both Hellenism and Eastern Orthodox Christianity. In many ways, the attempts by the Western Roman Empire to blend pagan practices and Christian beliefs together had floundered, leading to an identity crisis and a loss of morale. But where the Western Romans had failed, the Eastern Romans managed to succeed.

In the Byzantine Empire (a term that originated after its fall in 1453), you would find the best of both worlds. While rejecting the paganism of Hellenism, the Byzantines held onto much of the more rationale strains of Greek thought and philosophy and successfully adapted them to the scriptures of the Bible. In many ways, this syncretic blend of the Christian religion and Greek philosophy had already begun in the days of the Bible's New Testament.

After all, it was the Apostle Paul—often described as a "Hellenized Jew" who was versed in both the Greek language and culture—who famously traveled from Israel all the way to Greek lands, where he debated Greek philosophers face to face. However, Paul didn't just argue with the Greeks. He reasoned with them in their own fashion and once even quoted a famed Greek poet named Aratus just to prove a point.

Aratus had written a treatise on the erosion of the Greeks' traditional faith many years prior, and even though many had ceased to believe in the myths of old, Aratus had argued that the gods were not dead but alive and well. He said that it was in Zeus that the Greeks "live and move and have their being." Paul perfectly adapted this to Christian beliefs. He simply cut Zeus from the equation and quoted the words right back to the astonished Greeks.

As Paul actually states in the biblical Book of Acts, "'In him we live and move and have our being;' as even some of your own poets have said, 'For we are indeed his offspring.'" By quoting the words of a Greek poet, Paul masterfully blended Hellenism and Christianity into this verse from the Bible.

With this syncretic foundation set, the Byzantines were able to build on this tradition quite well. Whereas the Latin West tore down much of its Hellenistic past and faced an identity crisis after becoming Christian, the Greek East was able to create a rather smooth transition.

And it probably didn't hurt that the New Testament itself was originally written in Greek. For the Eastern Christians of the Balkans, no transliteration to Latin was required. At any rate, it was the strong bond of the Christian religion, overlaid on top of traditional Greek customs and traditions, that proved to be the formidable glue that held the Byzantine Empire together.

Throughout the Byzantine Empire, civil servants were highly educated both in classic Greek teachings, such as Socrates, Plato, and Aristotle, as well as the teachings of Christianity. The people held fast to both the spirituality of the Christian faith and the platonic wisdom of their Greek ancestors. Even their monumental church, the Hagia Sophia, seemed to encapsulate this merger.

The Greeks preserved their traditions, and fortunately for the rest of the world, their Ottoman conquerors would deem the Greek teachings valuable enough to save. They preserved it like a precious flame, as if they were waiting for western Europe's rediscovery of Greek values during the Renaissance centuries later.

Having said that, the Greek Byzantine culture would have a heavy hold on the Balkans for many centuries. Even after an invasion of the Slavic and Bulgar tribes knocked portions of the Balkan Peninsula out of the Byzantine orbit in the 7th century, the pull of Constantinople was strong. By the 13th century, the invaders would become Orthodox Christians. They would be transformed by the Byzantines of the Balkans rather than transforming and remaking the Balkans in their own image.

It was under Byzantine tutelage that many of the forerunner, proto-states of Balkan countries, such as Bosnia, Croatia, Hungary, Romania, Serbia, Slovenia, and Bulgaria, would come into being. But by the turn of the millennium, the Greek Orthodox Byzantines were not the only Christian powers vying for new converts. By the year 1000, the successor states of the Western Roman Empire had risen from the rubble and reconstituted themselves into several Catholic nation-states.

These states were politically divided and ruled by different potentates, but they had a thread of unity since ostensibly all of the Christian Latin West was under the religious authority of the pope in Rome. In this way, the pope could be said to have—at least in theory—replaced the Western Roman emperor as the overarching authority in the west.

Interestingly enough, this power structure was the opposite of the Byzantines in the east. In the Byzantine Empire, the Byzantine emperor was considered the absolute head of the church, with the top religious leader—the patriarch—ultimately subordinate to imperial decrees. The Byzantine emperor could dismiss the patriarch if they felt like it. In the west, no leader had the power to dismiss the pope. They could try to depose a pope through warfare and physical violence, but short of a military occupation, no western leader had the ability to simply sign off on a decree to have the pope immediately dismissed.

On the other hand, the pope, with just a wave of his hand, could have western leaders excommunicated from the church. And although this did nothing to the monarch's immediate temporal power, being blacklisted and essentially banned from the Catholic Church would have likely ruined their reputation.

At any rate, this difference in the power structures would end up being one of the main driving factors for the official split between the Roman Catholic and the Orthodox Church, which occurred in 1054. Once these pronounced differences set in, the Catholic West began to more aggressively send missionaries to convert the remaining pagans of the Balkans. This resulted in most of the residents of the southeastern Balkans, in proximity to the Byzantine Empire, converting to the Greek Orthodox faith, while those in the northwestern reaches of the Balkans converted to Roman Catholicism.

These divisions can still be found to this very day. Nations like Croatia and Slovenia are Catholic, whereas Macedonia, Serbia, and

Bulgaria are Orthodox. But whether they became Catholic or Orthodox, the new Christian converts in the Balkan interior usually kept many of their pagan traditions under the surface. This meant that previously pagan holidays were conveniently converted into celebrations of various saints and church-themed events.

The biggest influx of newcomers to the region were the Slavic tribes, which had begun coming south in the 6th century. Over time, these new settlers began to displace the original inhabitants, and the Byzantine reach into the Balkans was steadily reduced. Although the immigrants seemed like invaders at times, they did not come under one invading army. The Slavic tribes are said to have come in unorganized waves over the centuries.

The infiltration may not have had a centralized leader, but to the Byzantines on the receiving end, the effects were substantial. As Byzantine chronicler John of Ephesus puts it in an account he wrote in 585, "The accursed people—the Slavs—arose and passed through the whole of the Hellades, through Thessaly and Thrace conquering many towns and forts, wasted and burnt, looted. They overcame the country and settled it freely without fear as if it were their own, and strange to say to the present day inhabit it—and sit secure in the lands of the Romans without fear or cares. Plundering, murdering, and burning."

John of Ephesus was quite disgusted, not only that the Slavs conducted raids against the Byzantines but that they also decided to set down roots in the Balkans when they were done. The Byzantines were used to wandering nomads occasionally storming through, raiding their lands, and then taking off. For the Byzantines at the time, the idea that such troublemakers would actually stay was almost unheard-of.

But oddly enough, after they were done raiding, they settled down and began cultivating the land, growing their own food and herding their own flocks. Essentially, they transformed from wayward raiders to settled farmers of the Balkans in a very short period of time. It seems that after their brief spurt of violence, the Slavic newcomers hammered their swords into plow shears, and as a sign of goodwill, they began to marry among the locals.

They did assimilate with other Balkan peoples pretty quickly, utilizing their languages, adopting customs, and converting to the local religion. It would then be the settled Slavs and their descendants who would have to defend *their* territory from any would-be outside aggressors.

While the Slavs often adopted Christianity and other customs of the Byzantine-dominated Balkans, they also introduced some of their own beliefs. The Slavs, for example, carried over pagan superstition regarding various wilderness spirits and even ingrained the locals with a fear that the dead might somehow become vampires. The fear would become so ingrained that, on occasion, graves would actually be dug up just so worried locals could drive a stake through the heart of the deceased. Sometimes, they opted to cut off the head of the dead since post-mortem beheading was also believed to be a means of preventing vampirism.

No, this isn't a tale cooked up in Hollywood—these things actually happened. And anyone who has ever seen Dracula movies knows full well that the Balkans is the prime backdrop for vampire tales. Along with a belief in vampires, the Slavs also brought a rich tradition of finely crafted pottery, as well as metallurgy, to the Balkans. They knew how to forge plow shears, swords, knives, and daggers.

They also had a fondness for ornaments, as attested by the fact that they buried their dead with fine bracelets, rings, and other forms of jewelry. Taking this into consideration, grave robbery may have been an ulterior motive for digging up the dead rather than just checking for vampires. These newcomers to the Balkans lived in fairly simple houses that centered around a stone hearth, which was used for cooking and heating the home. The land immediately around this homestead was utilized for personal farming.

The Slavs maintained a rural presence in the Balkans while the older residents urbanized and began a steady migration toward the cities of Constantinople, Salonika, Split, Ragusa, Trogir, and Zadar. The Byzantine economy began to steadily retract at this point, with the Slavic newcomers relying more on subsistence farming rather than imperial largesse. As the Byzantine grip loosened over much of the Balkan provinces, Byzantine coins, which at one time were prevalent in the Balkans, became increasingly rare.

The Byzantines eventually regained much of their influence. By the time of Heraclius, who came to power in Byzantium in 610, much of the former glory of the Byzantine Empire had been restored. Byzantine traders began to make inroads back into the Balkan interior, where new forms of economic bartering began to take place. However, the Byzantine Empire would be terribly rocked right in the middle of the 7th century by the rise of Islam.

The Byzantines had just put down aggression from Persia. The Persian Empire had long rivaled Rome, and after a tremendous struggle, the Byzantines had finally defeated the Persians. It was right on the heels of this spectacular victory that the Byzantines were faced with the Islamic power that had arisen in Arabia.

These Muslim forces launched lightning strikes against Byzantine holdings in both the Levant and North Africa. The Byzantine economy and manpower had already been drained from the recent wars with Persia, so they were in no shape to cope with this massive incursion. The most they could do was to keep the invaders out of the Byzantine heartland in Asia Minor. But losing their territory in the Levant and North Africa was a devastating blow, not only to Byzantine prestige but also to the Byzantine economy.

The loss of revenue was staggering. And this loss, especially the loss of the breadbasket of Egypt, was felt in the Balkans, where surplus grain was always a welcome trade good. Nevertheless, even without their prized territory in the Levant and North Africa, the

Byzantines were able to steady themselves, and with time, much of this reorientation involved a much greater focus on the Balkans.

By the 12th century, business was booming, and mining had become an important industry in the Balkan interior. Mining towns, such as Srebrenica ("Silvertown") and Olovo ("Lead Town"), would seem to attest.

In the meantime, the Byzantine powerbrokers of the Balkans had developed a new enemy. A Turkic group originating from the eastern steppes of Mongolia and Xinjiang Province of China had established outposts in Asia Minor, and they were steadily growing in power. In fact, in 1071, this confederation of Turks managed to deal a decisive defeat to the Byzantines at the Battle of Manzikert. The defeat was so disastrous that the Byzantines temporarily lost control of Asia Minor.

It was this devastating loss that helped to instigate the First Crusade. Despite their differences, the pope in Rome took up the call to help the Eastern Christians, as well as to make a bid to recover the Holy Land, which had fallen to Muslim forces in the 7th century. It was actually shortly after the Muslim conquests of the Holy Land in the 7th century that Islam first reached the Turkic tribes of the steppes. A Turkic group called the Uyghurs were among the first to shed their traditional shamanistic religion in favor of Islam.

At any rate, by 1071, the Turks had seized many Byzantine settlements in eastern Asia Minor and were steadily pushing west. The Turks then met the Byzantine army at the climactic Battle of Manzikert, which was a Byzantine city. The Byzantines were defeated, and their own emperor—Romanus IV Diogenes—was taken as a prisoner of war.

John Doukas, who was considered the "de facto" administrator, ruling through Michael VII, went on the offensive against the Turks. It was a terrific struggle. Although some ground would be reclaimed, completely dislodging the Turks from eastern Asia Minor would prove an impossible task. The Turks inevitably continued to push west until they were once again in control of most of Asia Minor.

The Turks would rename their holdings the Sultanate of Rum, which was in reference to the fact that the lands used to belong to the Roman Empire. In 1095, Byzantine Emperor Alexius I Comnenus (also spelled as Alexios I Komnenos) broke down and requested help from the west. This request for aid led to the pope calling for the First Crusade.

Although a large portion of Asia Minor was regained with the aid of the Crusaders, the Turks would still cling to a huge chunk of eastern Asia Minor. The Crusaders were successful in establishing Crusader states in the Levant, which more or less served as a buffer state between the Byzantines and their many enemies.

But the Crusaders themselves, after a series of military defeats, were ultimately expelled from the region at the end of the 13th century. Even worse, as relations between the Latin West and the Orthodox East broke down, the Crusaders had turned on the Byzantines. In 1204, they actually sacked the capital of Constantinople. The Byzantines eventually regained control, but they were never quite the same, and their decline was hastened by a considerable degree.

At any rate, by the 1300s, a weakened Byzantine Empire was left to face the encroaching Turks by itself. In the 1300s, the resurgent groups were being led by a man named Osman. He was also sometimes referred to as Othman, and it was from his name that this particular group of Turks came to be known as the "Ottomans." Under Osman, the Ottoman Turks laid siege to Nicaea in 1301 and managed to capture Bursa in 1326. Nicaea itself fell a few years later in 1331. This was followed by the fall of Nicomedia in 1337.

With every victory, the Ottoman Turks were inching steadily closer to the very gates of Constantinople. They were also pushing even farther into the Balkans. By this time, distinct Balkan states were beginning to form in their own right. Chief among these was the proto-kingdom of Bulgaria, which was established by the Bulgars.

The Bulgars first appeared in Byzantine territory in the 7th century. They typically stayed near the vicinity of Constantinople. In 681, a

Bulgar leader named Isperikh (also spelled as Asparukh or Asparuh) was actually able to bully the Byzantines into granting the Bulgars territory in the southern reaches of the Danube River. From this settlement, a massive kingdom would develop, and it comprised a large chunk of the Balkans.

The Bulgarians then began to enter into Byzantine power politics in a big way. In 705 CE, they even managed to aid a previously exiled Byzantine emperor—Justinian II—regain his throne. Justinian had courted the wrath of the general public through high taxes, and the elite disliked him due to his attempts to reform the civil service. This emperor-in-exile had been tossed out due to the increasingly fickle factions within Byzantium itself. Yet, once exiled to the Balkans, Justinian II managed to rally a large Bulgarian force with the help of a Bulgarian warlord named Han Tervel. He used them to march on Constantinople.

It would have been nice if this Christian monarch could have just forgiven and forgotten about the transgressions of his political opponents. But this was not the case. In fact, one account states that when he and his comrades were crossing the Black Sea, after encountering turbulent weather, a frightened colleague suggested that if Justinian perhaps swore an oath to have mercy on his foes, the storm would cease. To this, Justinian II allegedly snapped back, "If I spare a single one of them, may God drown me here."

And as soon as he clawed his way back to power, he kicked off a "reign of terror" against those who had opposed him. However, the crackdown was so brutal that rather than silencing the opposition, it emboldened them. By 711, this Byzantine potentate was taken down once again. And this time, his opponents would make sure that the deposed emperor would be gone for good by having him executed.

Perhaps taking their cue from their Slavic neighbors, who often warned that the dead could rise lest they were beheaded or had a stake driven into their hearts, the Byzantines chopped Justinian II's head off. The Bulgars would once again emerge when Constantinople was besieged by Islamic forces in 717.

The defense of the city was overseen by the latest man to claim the Byzantine throne, Emperor Leo III. Leo ingeniously had his navy meet the invading ships head-on, where they unleashed Byzantium's greatest secret weapon, a little something called "Greek fire." They launched a fiery kind of napalm through specially outfitted copper tubes, and the invaders were incinerated.

A Bulgarian army from the Balkans, tens of thousands strong, then managed to mop up the lingering enemy troops on land. The Bulgars of the Balkans would not remain allies for long, though, and Leo's own successor, Constantine V, would end up battling against them and perishing during a major offensive in the Balkans in 775. The Byzantine who would truly give the Bulgars a run for their money, however, was Emperor Basil II or, as he was better known, the Bulgar Slayer.

Basil very much lived up to that name. Under his ruthless command, a resurgent Byzantine force swept through the Balkan Peninsula and once again made it their own. By the time the Bulgar Slayer perished in 1025, the Byzantines were the undisputed masters of the Balkans once again. In the next few decades, Byzantium's attention would once again be drawn to its southern flanks, as a Turkic tribe known as the Seljuks began to rise up against them. The situation then came to a head at the Battle of Manzikert in 1071.

As mentioned earlier, the Byzantines suffered a terrible defeat, and the emperor—Romanus Diogenes—was taken hostage. However, the Turks proved rather magnanimous, and once the emperor agreed to certain territorial concessions, they actually allowed the emperor to return to Constantinople. His fellow Byzantines were enraged at the deal the emperor had struck, though, and he was deposed. His successors proved unable to stave off the Turkish advance, and by 1100, much of Asia Minor had been lost, leaving the Balkans as the primary Byzantine domain.

However, it is important to note that the Byzantines did not dominate the Balkans completely. At this time, an early Croatian kingdom had come to prominence in the northwest of the Balkan Peninsula. The Kingdom of Croatia, which was situated just across the Adriatic Sea from Catholic Italy, was always more closely aligned with the Catholic West than the Orthodox East. And the fact that Croatians today are still predominantly Catholic is a good testament to this legacy.

By 1102, however, there was a shift in power in the Balkans, and the Magyar tribe, which predated the modern-day Hungarians, took control of the region. The Magyars would end up being the last of the migrants to rush into the Balkans from the north and take up shop on a permanent basis. Their territory contained land that is considered to be outside of the Balkans, but they also held the northwestern reaches of the Balkan Peninsula.

In particular, they had hegemony over the lands of Croatia, most of Bosnia, chunks of modern-day Slovakia, and what would today be considered Transylvania. Although they were usurpers, the Byzantines, with time and a combination of military force and political diplomacy, were able to bring the restless Magyars into their political orbit as well, thereby securing the Byzantines' Balkan backyard once again.

The tribal groups of the Balkans, despite their own personal aspirations, couldn't help but be overawed by the Byzantines, and the road to becoming client states was all but inevitable. However, by the 1300s, a resurgent group of Turks—that Turkic group that would come to be known as the Ottomans—would trample through the Balkans and disturb this delicate balance.

Due to their conquests in the Balkans, the Ottomans would come to almost completely outflank Constantinople. For a time, all that prevented this bright, shining Byzantine beacon of the Balkans from complete and utter collapse was Constantinople's thick Theodosian Walls.

Chapter 4 – The Balkans under Ottoman Occupation

"A history of perceived humiliation, after all, lurks behind many acts of terror. And competing narratives of victimhood and insults sustain conflicts in the Balkans, the Caucasus, the Middle East and many other regions."

-Serge Schmemann

The origins of the Ottoman Empire can be traced back to a powerful Turkish warlord by the name of Osman Bey. Osman, whose name was often corrupted into Othman, would lend his name to the term "Ottoman Empire." The Turkish followers of Osman would first diverge from the previous Turkish powerbrokers in Anatolia—the Seljuk Turks—in 1299.

From then on, their power would only grow. While other Turkish groups were squabbling amongst each other in Asia Minor, this particular confederacy gained steam and began to assert itself in Anatolia and then ultimately in the Balkans itself. The Ottomans began with just a small enclave in northwestern Asia Minor, but by 1326, they had seized the strategic outpost of Bursa. This was then followed up by a much greater prize, the Byzantine metropolis of

Nicaea, which was captured in 1331. Surging forward, the Ottoman Turks then took Nicomedia in 1337.

In the meantime, Constantinople was in rapid decline. The coffers were threadbare from having to fund constant military campaigns, and it seemed as if no end was in sight. Even worse, by the 1350s, the Byzantines began to fight each other. A civil war broke out when two co-emperors—John Palaeologus (Palaiologos) and John Cantacuzenus (Kantakouzenos)—began battling each other.

Both men needed auxiliary forces to aid their cause. Palaeologus enlisted the Serbs, while Cantacuzenus actually tapped the Ottoman Turks for assistance. It was during this infighting that the Ottomans first made their way over the Dardanelles and onto European soil. Incredibly enough, shortly after their arrival, a literal earthquake erupted, causing extensive damage to the city walls of Gallipoli.

The Turks—as just about anyone from the Middle Ages might have done—interpreted the event as a miraculous sign. They believed that the tumbling of the walls was a supernatural event that demonstrated that Allah was on their side. And taking the initiative, the Ottomans were able to successfully capture the famed Byzantine town of Adrianople in 1361, which they subsequently called Edirne. From their new base in the southern reaches of the Balkan Peninsula, the Ottomans would plot future Balkan campaigns. And soon enough, Constantinople itself was in a chokehold, with energetic Turkish forces closing in on both sides of the Bosporus Strait.

However, before the Ottomans could take Constantinople, they had to contend with the Serbs. The Ottomans might have been growing and expanding at the expense of Byzantine weakness, but so had the Serbs. Just north of the contracted Byzantine lands, the Serbs were attempting to build up their own powerful kingdom in the Balkans under their leader Stephen Dushan (Stefen Dušan). The Serbs had seized Albania, Thrace, and much of Macedonia.

In fact, in 1346, Stephen Dushan had actually gone as far as to declare himself to be the "Emperor of the Serbs and Greeks."

Stephen Dushan's aspirations went even further than that. He had dreams of one day sitting on the throne in Constantinople. He also reached out to western powers—in particular the Venetians—and highlighted a scheme in which he would seize power from the Byzantines and unite the Western and Eastern churches as one. This grandiose plan never came to fruition, however, as Stephen abruptly perished in 1355.

Nevertheless, if the Ottomans wanted to take out the last vestiges of the Byzantine Empire, they would have to take on the Serbs. And by the time the Ottomans were pushing into the Balkans in the early 1360s, the power base of the Serbs was strong enough to give them a hard time.

After the Ottomans seized control of the city of Philippopolis in 1363, the Serbs and the Ottoman Turks were on the verge of a major confrontation. The Byzantine Empire had held back the Ottomans from the Balkans for centuries, but Balkan residents now had to contend with these infiltrators on their own. Realizing the danger they faced, Balkan tribes began to band together in order to present a united front against the invading Ottomans. This resulted in a large army of Serbs, Wallachians, Hungarians, and Bosnians, who all came together to defend their lands.

Initially, this group presented a formidable threat to the Ottoman advance. But it seems that perhaps this Balkan brigade didn't take things seriously enough. It has been said that since the Balkan forces had the initial edge, after a few days' march, they settled down near Turkish positions and actually began to engage in a hearty celebration. Since they had not won anything yet, it remains unclear exactly what they were celebrating. But the Turks apparently got word of the festivities and decided it was a good time to strike while their enemies were nearby gorging themselves with food and getting drunk on wine.

The Ottomans struck after nightfall, finding the enemy sound asleep. Upon their rude awakening, this hungover Balkan force attempted to make an unorganized retreat over the Maritza River, where a large contingent of their number tripped and fell into their own watery grave. This was the first major confrontation between the Ottomans and the local Balkan defenders, and it seemed to set the stage for what was to come.

By 1365, the Ottomans had made Edirne their official capital and their forward base of operations against their foes in the Balkans. And even though the Ottomans were at odds with the Balkan people, there were still occasions in which political alliances of convenience could be forged in the complex political landscape of the Balkan Peninsula. In 1365, Bulgaria teamed up with the Turks.

In the midst of this alliance, the Byzantine emperor just happened to make his way through Bulgarian lands and ended up getting taken prisoner by the Bulgarians. The following year, the Latin pope called for a crusade to rid the Balkans of the Turks. The call was met by the kidnapped Byzantine ruler's own cousin, Duke Amadeus VI of Savoy.

The duke led his navy across the Aegean Sea and into the Dardanelles. After a fierce struggle, he managed to seize Gallipoli from the Ottomans. Amadeus VI also managed to free his cousin, the emperor himself, after conducting a raid on the Bulgarians. Bulgarian power significantly declined after this series of events, and their one-time ally, the Ottomans, gained the upper hand.

This set the stage for the Battle of Samokov, in which the Ottomans flung aside their previous alliance and took Bulgarian lands by force. This dominion went largely unchallenged until 1388. That year, Ottoman Sultan Murad I was busy skirmishing in Asia Minor. A confederation of Bulgarians, Serbs, Bosnians, Albanians, and Wallachians all came together and attempted to push the Turks out by launching a major offensive.

The following year, Murad was back with a vengeance. Along with his mighty Turkish cavalry, he had large contingents of local troops made up of Serbs, Bulgarians, and Albanians, which had defected to the Ottoman side. These forces clashed with the pro-Balkan independence coalition on June 28th, 1389, in Kosovo. A terrific battle ensued, but in the end, the Turks were able to defeat their opponents.

Nevertheless, the victory was bittersweet since Sultan Murad I perished during the onslaught. Sultan Murad was apparently not killed in the battle. He was actually assassinated by a Serbian nationalist that had slipped into the Ottoman camp. Although the account is sometimes called into question, according to Serbian tradition, the assassin was a man named Milos Obilic, who, after being accused of cowardice, decided to show his bravery by singlehandedly taking out the leader of the Ottomans himself.

It certainly must have taken quite a bit of courage for a man to sneak behind enemy lines and then walk right up to the leader of the enemy encampment and kill him. Chillingly enough, Serbian assassins would play a big part in the history of this region in the years to come. After all, the First World War was infamously instigated by a Serbian assassin in the Balkans.

But as it pertains to this particular episode of assassination, it is not clear exactly what happened to Murad's killer after the hit was made. At any rate, Murad's death did absolutely nothing to stop the Turkish machine, as it was able to march on just fine with Murad's successor, Bayezid I, who immediately became the new sultan upon Murad's demise.

Shortly thereafter, the Serbian leader, Lazar, was taken hostage, and he was ultimately killed as a point of pure and simple vengeance. His son, Stephen Lazarevic, went on to succeed his father. Despite his father's murder at the hands of the Turks, he went on to become an obedient puppet ruler in the Balkans who towed the lines for the Ottomans. By 1393, the Ottomans under Sultan Bayezid managed to capture the last chunk of free and independent Bulgaria. Bosnia had also submitted in 1391.

The Ottomans continued to push into the Balkans, and in 1395, they managed to defeat the forces of Wallachia, which were led by a Wallachian prince, Mircea. Curiously, the Ottomans left Mircea in place, apparently hoping that they could rely on him to be an obedient client ruler, just as they had done with Stephen Lazarevic. But Mircea was not going to be anyone's stooge. As soon as he had the chance, he took off to Hungary in the north, where he entreated the Hungarian king, Sigismund, to cobble together a resistance force to take on the Ottomans.

This request for aid resulted in a mini-crusade, in which Hungary, the pope, the duke of Burgundy, and small contributions from France and Germany all came together to take on the Ottoman threat. The primary objective of Prince Mircea was merely to get back Wallachia, but the European authorities leading this charge had a mightier aim, one of rescuing Constantinople, which at that point was surrounded and under a blockade by the Ottomans.

This Christian coalition of European troops came together at the Hungarian city of Buda and then charged south, following the Danube River. However, these Christian forces got a bit sidetracked when they began looting fellow Christian outposts they met along the way. It has been said that two Bulgarian settlements were sacked before the Crusaders even came anywhere near the Ottoman encampment.

There is, of course, no excuse for such wanton violence, and it is depredations such as this that would go on to mar the more noble sensibilities of the Crusaders. Their mission at the start was often a high and lofty one of saving Christian brethren who were under siege, but the actions of Christian troops often left much to be desired.

At any rate, in the Ottoman-occupied city of Nicopolis, the Crusaders first encountered the Turks. As soon as they came face to face with the mighty walls of this city, the Crusaders realized they had made a grave mistake. They were ready for a battle out in the open, but they had no siege equipment to help them break into a walled city. As such, they were forced to camp outside of the city walls, seemingly unable to advance any further.

Bored and listless, many of the troops began to play games with each other, such as jousts and other activities. Perhaps the Crusaders were so desperate to get attention that they created a spectacle to draw in the Turkish forces. If so, they were successful.

It did not take long for Sultan Bayezid, who was near Constantinople, to be alerted to the intrusion, and he sent his forces to intercept the interlopers. This force actually included a large contingent of Serbian cavalry, which was led by none other than the puppet ruler Stephen Lazarevic.

On the opposing side was King Sigismund of Hungary, who led the charge by sending in highly mobile archers on horseback. The archers were sent in to soften up the front lines and probe for weaknesses. After this wave of archers was launched, the heavily armed units of infantry were sent rushing in to engage the Ottoman forces directly.

However, the zeal held among the Christian knights was so great that it actually led to competition. And the French knights were so determined to get to the enemy first that they charged ahead of the rest. This was a terrible mistake. In their haste, the French had exposed their flanks to attack and were soon cut down as the Ottomans closed in. It has been said that the king of Hungary was not quite sure what had happened to the French contingent of knights until he saw a "stampede of wounded and riderless" steeds rush past the Hungarian forces.

Nevertheless, Sigismund tried to recoup and sent his Hungarian infantry to meet the enemy. It was just then that the Serbian cavalry under Lazarevic was unleashed upon the Hungarians. The Serbs managed to break the Hungarian lines and forced them into a disorganized retreat back to their transport craft, which had been left on the banks of the Danube. It was a chaotic scene, one in which the defeated Crusaders actually began to fight each other over access to the boats.

In all, it was a spectacular victory for the Ottoman forces. Bayezid could have gone on to take his place as an honorable champion of the

Turkish cause, but he could not resist delving out reprisals. He was apparently irked at the high cost of resources and lives that his own troops had sustained to achieve their victory over the Crusaders. He had also received reports of the abuse that the Crusaders had heaped upon local residents.

This was apparently enough for the sultan to determine that revenge was in order. With the rare exception of a few, such as Jean de Nevers—the duke of Burgundy's son—there would be no quarter for the prisoners of war who found themselves held hostage at the Ottoman camp, at least for the most part. Another lucky survivor who found mercy was a man by the name of Johann Schiltberger. He was apparently quite young at the time of his capture, and someone decided to show the boy mercy and spare his life.

This allowed Schiltberger to later recall what happened following the defeat of the Crusader contingent. According to Schiltberger, "Then each was ordered to kill his own prisoners, and for those who did not wish to do so, the king [sultan] appointed others in their place. Then they took my companions and cut off their heads, and when it came to my turn, the king's son saw me and ordered that I should be left alive, and I was taken to the other boys, because none under 20 years of age were killed, and I was scarcely 16 years old."

The defeat of the Crusader force was not only demoralizing for the Crusaders but also for Constantinople. The Byzantine authorities began to realize just how isolated they were. The dire situation of being surrounded by the Ottomans led Byzantine Emperor Manuel II to actually sneak out of the city in 1399 to directly appeal to the European powers of the west for aid.

After the disastrous defeat of Sigismund's coalition, he was hard-pressed to get any takers. However, Manuel II would end up receiving assistance from an entirely unexpected source, as the Ottomans suddenly found themselves under attack on their eastern Anatolian flank by a Mongol warlord named Tamerlane. The threat of the Mongol forces was so great that Bayezid was forced to call off the ongoing siege of Constantinople and redirect the vast bulk of his army toward Tamerlane's horde in the east.

Because just as the Ottomans were threatening the capital of the Byzantine Empire, the Mongols were threatening the capital of the Ottoman Empire, Ankara. Tamerlane's troops ended up camping just outside of Ankara's walls. Ironically, it was the mighty walls of this former Byzantine city that proved to be the best safeguard against Tamerlane's forces, as they were unable to immediately overrun the city.

The fortifications managed to delay the Mongol attackers long enough for Bayezid's reinforcements to arrive. It was then, right out in the open, outside of the gates of Ankara, that a large Ottoman army faced off against an equally massive army of Mongols. During this epic battle, the auxiliary Balkan forces led by Lazarevic managed to take the initiative.

The Serbian cavalry once again charged, sending the left flank of Tamerlane's troops into a panic. Sultan Bayezid had a major problem on his hands because a significant chunk of his troops, who were related to the Mongols, began to defect to Tamerlane's side. This led to the Ottoman army—at least those who remained loyal—to essentially be pilloried from both their front and rear flanks, as those who defected began to stab their comrades quite literally in the back.

The onslaught was so intense that the Serbian cavalry was forced to retreat. Sultan Bayezid himself came into jeopardy, as his forces were steadily reduced until it was just a basic corps of troops around his own person. Defeated, the sultan managed to break through the enemy lines with just a few hundred troops and take flight. While the sultan had been turned into a refugee in his own domain, Tamerlane took hold of Ankara and proceeded to loot nearby towns, such as Bursa, where a tremendous amount of wealth was seized by the Mongols.

Tamerlane eventually tracked down Bayezid and took him prisoner. Bayezid would ultimately die in captivity, ushering in a new crisis of succession. The situation was so dire for the Ottomans that it almost appeared as if the entire Ottoman Empire was about to collapse.

The western powers, in the meantime, were beginning to take notice of Tamerlane, and they realized that it would not be long before he would reach out and strike them as well. And shortly after the Ottoman defeat, Tamerlane's forces managed to reach Smyrna in northwest Asia Minor, which had previously been occupied by the Knights Hospitaller, a Christian Crusading order. The Knights Hospitaller were unable to withstand the onslaught and were driven out.

The nearby powerbrokers in Venice saw these developments and came to realize that the Ottoman Turks were perhaps the lesser of two evils. As such, they actually began to aid the weakened Ottoman Empire against Tamerlane. The Venetians sent their own craft to transport fleeing Ottoman troops to Thrace in the Balkans, where they were able to lick their wounds and regroup.

However, as fearsome as Tamerlane was in battle, the civil infrastructure he left behind in his sprawling empire was not the best. So, whenever his back was turned, there was always a threat of insurrection and revolt.

Just as Tamerlane was preparing to pursue the Ottomans into the Balkans, he received word that his holdings in Iraq were in jeopardy. This news sent Tamerlane charging to the Middle East and thereby diverting the Mongols from taking any action in the Balkans. Tamerlane then headed farther east in an attempt to subdue the Chinese; he would perish in the attempt, dying in 1404.

The threat of complete and utter annihilation at the hands of Tamerlane had been narrowly averted by the Ottomans. But in the meantime, the shattered Ottoman Empire had been rendered rudderless. The Ottomans were completely adrift without a solid, unifying leader. Infighting among the Ottomans ensued before a new leader by the name of Mehmed I rose to power in 1411.

Mehmed had to spend the next few years consolidating his gains, putting down the final resistance to his rule in 1413. Weakened by the infighting, Mehmed attempted to strengthen his position diplomatically by forging several alliances in the Balkans, which included strengthening ties with both the Byzantine Empire and the Serbian powerbrokers in the region. Mehmed, who would go down in Ottoman history as the "Great Restorer," was indeed able to revive the shattered Ottoman Empire.

By the time of his demise in 1421, Ottoman power was on the rebound once again. In fact, his ambitious heir Sultan Murad II was able to make the best of his predecessor's gains and almost immediately went on the offensive. Murad II would actually decide to turn against the Ottoman Empire's former ally, the Byzantines, in order to attempt a renewed siege of the Byzantine capital of Constantinople.

Sultan Murad's decision to attack Constantinople was both in the spirit of conquest, as well as out of irritation over continuous Byzantine plotting and intrigue. The Byzantine Empire was playing an extremely weak hand at this point, and it often resorted to various tactics of deception in order to keep the Ottomans off balance. The Byzantines had perfected the art of playing their enemies against each other, and Sultan Murad was sick of it.

It was said that whenever there was any dissent in the Ottoman ranks or if a rival to the sultan rose up, Murad could sense that a "Byzantine hand" was behind it. Part of this might have been imagined on Murad's part, but there can be no doubt that the Byzantines desired the Ottomans to remain fractured and plagued by internal turmoil since their infighting served Byzantine interests. And when Murad laid siege to Constantinople in 1422, the Byzantines did indeed have a trick up their sleeve.

When Murad was right at the gates of the city, the Byzantines set Murad's brother Mustafa, whom they were holding as a prisoner of war, free. They did this to distract the sultan and sow chaos in the ranks. And it worked. As soon as Mustafa was set loose, he headed off to loyal factions in Anatolia and mounted a rebellion against Murad. The tumult was enough to force Murad to call off the siege of Constantinople.

At this time, the Byzantines had yet another ace up their sleeve in the form of a paid insider, Murad's own chief vizier Halil Pasha. As it turns out, Pasha was on the payroll of the Byzantines, even though he had the ear of the Ottoman sultan. It was Pasha, under the direction of the Byzantines, who managed to persuade the sultan to call off his plans to invade Constantinople. Pasha had been whispering rumors into his ears that such an assault would unite the European Christian kingdoms and unleash a massive Crusade against the Turks.

The sultan listened to the advice and entered into a period of peace with the Byzantines. Instead of laying siege to Constantinople, the sultan turned his attention to securing more terrain in the Balkan interior. In 1430, he led a campaign against Albania and Macedonia and skirmished all the way up to the Hungarian borderlands. These incursions led the Hungarian champion—John Hunyadi—to rise up against the Turks. And when Murad's forces seized the Castle of Smederevo just a short distance from Belgrade, John Hunyadi joined forces with the subsequently refugeed George Brankovic, the so-called "Despot of Serbia," to raise a large force to counterattack the Ottoman advance.

A joint Serbian/Hungarian contingent came down on Smederevo and took the Ottoman occupiers by surprise. John Hunyadi unleashed a vicious infantry assault while the cavalry circled the outskirts of the fighting, attacking the Turks on all sides. This approach was the opposite of the usual military tactic of sending in the cavalry units first. The unorthodox approach managed to knock the Turks completely off balance, and the Castle of Smederevo was successfully retaken.

It was said that in gratitude for the repatriation of his fortress, George Brankovic, Despot of Serbia, actually gifted John Hunyadi with the city of Belgrade. It would not be the first or the last time that Belgrade had fallen into Hungarian hands. Just a few years later, Hyundai would answer the call to defend the Balkans once again when the region of Transylvania came under assault by the Ottomans in 1442.

In the foreground of all this was a Wallachian prince by the name of Vlad II. Vlad was a knight in the service of the Order of the Dragon. It was due to this distinction that he was referred to as Vlad Dracul. He was also often simply called Dracul. Dracul, as you might have inferred, is an old Romanian term for "Dragon."

Interestingly enough, it would be Vlad II's son, Vlad III, who would be known as "Dracula" or the "Son of the Dragon." Yes, Vlad III, sometimes also known as "Vlad the Impaler," was indeed the infamous inspiration for the subsequent horror novels and movies about a supernatural vampiric count from the Balkans named Dracula.

But before we talk about the exploits of the "Son of the Dragon," let us discuss his father, Vlad II, first. As the ruler of Wallachia, Vlad Dracul was in a very precarious position, as he was on the front lines of the struggle against the Ottoman Empire. He had been aligned with the Holy Roman emperor—the ruler of a conglomerate of states in western and central Europe—but after the Holy Roman emperor abruptly passed in 1437, Vlad Dracul sensed that he was treading on some very thin ice.

As such, he actually reached out to the Ottomans in 1437 to sign a secret deal with them. If other Christian leaders knew about this arrangement, they would have considered it a damnable deal since Vlad Dracul had already sworn an oath to the Holy Roman emperor and the Christian cause in general. In fact, it was his oath to the Holy Roman emperor that had brought Vlad II into the Order of the Dragon. With this oath, he had promised to do everything he could to uphold and safeguard Christianity in the Balkans.

However, his back was up against the wall. Vlad Dracul felt he had no choice but to go back on his oath. For some of the more superstitious, this decision led Vlad Dracul to become cursed. And this notion that Vlad Dracul and subsequently his son, Vlad Dracula, had become cursed for the breaking of a holy oath would later become a part of the fiction and folklore surrounding the Dracula name.

Vlad Dracul felt he was doing all he could to prevent his kingdom from being annihilated by the Ottomans, but some believed that he had sold his soul to the devil by doing so. At any rate, in 1442, John Hunyadi led a combined force of warriors to take on the Turks. To the shock of his Christian cohorts, the Wallachian ruler Vlad Dracul suddenly stepped aside and allowed the Ottoman army to pass right through his lands so that they could charge right into the flanks of Hunyadi's standing army in Transylvania.

The assault caught the troops off guard, but John Hunyadi was able to recoup and ultimately lead his men to victory. At one point, he actually feigned a retreat, tricking the Turks into following his troops as they withdrew from the battlefield. However, this was only a ruse, and Hunyadi's forces were then able to snap back in place and outflank the Turks, cutting them to pieces in the bloody melee that ensued.

After the Turkish threat to Transylvania was put down, Hunyadi made his way to Wallachia to take on Vlad Dracul. Vlad Dracul was not about to sit around and become captured, as he knew full well that the penalty for his treachery against Hunyadi would most likely be death. As such, Vlad fled to Ottoman territory, where he would remain as a refugee. In the meantime, the principality of Wallachia would be handed off to a Hungarian ally by the name of Basarab II.

Vlad Dracul bided his time with the Turks in Asia Minor until 1443. After further conquest, the Ottomans were able to forcibly reinstall Vlad Dracul as their puppet ruler in Wallachia. According to the terms of the deal, Vlad Dracul had to pay annual monetary tributes to the sultan, as well as provide young men to be sent off to join the Ottoman army.

John Hunyadi and his forces were gathering steam, and they were resolute in their mission to roll back Ottoman gains in the Balkans. In November of 1443, this force was able to take the Ottoman-occupied Serbian city of Nis. After the capture of Nis, Hunyadi's army then passed through the Balkan Mountains before catching up with a contingent of Turkish troops on Christmas Day. The Ottomans were once again defeated, but at this point, Hunyadi's men began to face a lack of proper food and water. Hunyadi made a tactical withdrawal, arriving at the city of Buda in February of 1444.

Nevertheless, the chastisement he had given the Turks was severe enough that Murad II was convinced to enter into a ten-year truce with the Hungarians. Hunyadi had succeeded in halting the Turkish advance in the Balkan interior. But due to political intrigue, the ten-year truce would prove to be worthless. Some in western Europe, encouraged by the major victories of Hunyadi, were calling for nothing short of another Crusade. Leading this charge was a certain cardinal whose name comes down to us as Cesarini. He was convinced that the time was ripe for a massive Crusader force to put the Ottoman Turks out of business entirely. The good cardinal furthermore proclaimed that the treaty with the Turks should be considered null and void since no treaty signed with "infidels" was worth honoring.

So, a new force led by Hungary was cobbled together in the summer of 1444, and it was led into Bulgaria to take on the Ottomans once again. The sultan, however, was prepared. As it turns out, he did not even need the ten-year truce; just a few months of peace had been enough time for him to finish mopping up other outbreaks of fighting that had occurred in the far-flung regions of the Ottoman Empire. He could now focus the full might of his forces on the Balkan interior once more.

Interestingly enough, the sultan's former vassal, Vlad Dracul, had switched sides again. He was now openly aiding John Hunyadi's troops against the Turks. It seems that despite the previous bad blood, his promise of aid was enough for Hunyadi to simply let bygones be bygones. For Vlad II, the stakes could not have been higher. His two sons, Vlad III and Radu, were being held as royal hostages of the sultan. Just a word from the sultan could have ended their lives, yet Vlad Dracul nevertheless decided to return to the previous pledge he had made when he was sworn into the Order of the Dragon. Perhaps it was his last act of vindication, but he certainly did so with a heavy heart. Vlad Dracul even remarked at one point that he was absolutely certain that Vlad and Radu were doomed to be "butchered for the Christian peace." Perhaps it was because of this perceived sacrifice that Vlad Dracul's Christian cohorts were so forgiving of him.

In the end, the Christian Crusaders were decisively defeated at the Battle of Varna that November. Not only were the Hungarians defeated, but the king of Hungary and Croatia (as well as Poland), Vladislav III, was also killed in combat. It was a devastating blow, and it would prove to be a major turning point in the Balkans.

As it pertains to the Machiavellian character of Vlad Dracul, miraculously enough, the sultan would ultimately decide not to harm the children, regardless of their father's treachery. The sultan would use Vlad Dracul's kids as a bargaining chip to get him to turn on his Christian comrades once again, though. This resulted in Vlad Dracul signing yet another treaty with the Ottomans in 1447. The treaty had a sickening implication. As part of it, the sultan ordered Vlad Dracul to hand over thousands of Bulgarians who had sought refuge in his kingdom. Vlad Dracul knew that sending these beleaguered souls back to what was now Ottoman-occupied territory meant that he was consigning them to a life of slavery or worse. Nevertheless, Vlad Dracul did as he was commanded.

After John Hunyadi heard of this outrage, he gathered up what forces he could and stormed Vlad Dracul's castle in Wallachia. Vlad

Dracul attempted to escape, but he was seized when he tried to flee to Bucharest. He was summarily executed a short time later. Hunyadi then declared himself the new "Prince of Wallachia," but he would ultimately hand over the throne to yet another noble in waiting, Vladislav II.

Upon hearing of Vlad Dracul's demise, the sultan seemed to actually feel sorry for Dracul's newly orphaned children. He showed great compassion for the youths and made sure that their needs were taken care of by his own court. Vlad III—later known as Vlad Dracula—was even recruited to train with the Ottoman troops. The sultan was actually grooming the young Dracula to one day take back Wallachia and restore its client kingdom status to the Ottoman Empire.

But before we jump into what happened with Vlad Dracula, we have to look at the state of the Balkans before he took the throne. After the defeat of Varna in 1444, Pope Nicholas V called for yet another Crusade. Few would take him up on this call, but one enthusiastic supporter came in the form of George Skanderbeg of Albania. George raised an army and drew the full wrath of the Ottomans to Albania. John Hunyadi, with an army of primarily Hungarians and Wallachians, came rushing to the Albanians' aid. The Wallachians were led by the man that John Hunyadi had installed on the Wallachian throne in place of Vlad Dracul, Vladislav II. After crossing the Danube, the forces headed toward Kosovo. A protracted and bloody struggle ensued, but the Turkish troops, which greatly outnumbered the allied Crusaders, ultimately won.

With this threat from the Balkan interior temporarily put down, the Ottomans began to return their gaze to that fabled city of Byzantine brilliance—Constantinople. Murad II would pass away in 1451, but his son, Mehmed II, would succeed him and soon go on the offensive. The Byzantines, who had enjoyed relatively peaceful relations with the previous sultan, initially attempted to get on the new Turkish potentate's good side. Upon hearing of his arrival on the throne, Byzantine Emperor Constantine XI Palaeologus was quick to send over his congratulations.

The new sultan sent back friendly entreaties, pledging to continue the peaceful relations that his father had established at the end of his reign. But it wasn't long before relations would sour, and the Byzantines managed to provoke Mehmed's wrath. The Byzantines had been holding a member of the Turkish court—Prince Orhan—as a royal hostage. This was not what made Mehmed angry; the Ottomans were happy to be rid of a man they viewed as a dynastic troublemaker. In fact, Mehmed's father had been paying the Byzantines money to take care of Orhan and keep him under house arrest.

However, it seems the Byzantines were hoping to cash in, as they sent out a request for more money for the prince's upkeep. Writer and Byzantine historian Richard Fidler describes this request as essentially an attempt at blackmail on the Byzantines' part. They hoped that the young new Ottoman ruler would be like putty in their hands, allowing them to extract the most that they could from the bargaining chip in their possession.

Mehmed was not to be toyed with. Unlike his father, who had patiently dealt with Byzantine intrigue for decades, Mehmed began to make preparations for a full-scale offensive against the last vestige of the Byzantine Empire.

In the spring of 1452, Mehmed sent a small army of Turkish engineers to work just across the Bosporus Strait. These men were tasked with constructing a new formidable fortress that would be located just a few miles from Constantinople itself. This would be the base from which the siege of Constantinople would be launched. The Turks also already had an older fortress on the other side of the Bosporus Strait in Anatolia. Having fortified locations on each side of the strait would allow the Ottomans to better oversee a blockade.

This stranglehold on the strait was finalized by the following fall. This was demonstrated in November when a Venetian craft attempting to ferry supplies to the beleaguered Byzantines was blown out of the water by Turkish cannons positioned on either side of the strait. Constantinople was entirely cut off from the outside world as a massive army was being prepared just a short distance away to storm its walls.

In March of 1453, this army, backed by Turkish craft in the nearby waters, showed up at the very gates of Constantinople. Realizing that bargaining with the Turks was at an end, Emperor Constantine sent a final letter to Sultan Mehmed. The missive read, in part, "I take refuge in God. If he had decreed and decided to hand over this city to you, who can contradict him or prevent it? If he instills the idea of peace in your mind, I would gladly agree. For the moment, now that you have broken the treaties to which I am bound by oath, let these be dissolved. Henceforth I will keep the city gates closed. I will fight for the inhabitants with all my strength."

Despite the closed gates, the Ottomans came loaded for war. They had brought the latest in cannon technology—huge massive guns that they would use to pulverize the walls of Constantinople. One of them was said to be so big that it took a veritable army just to transport it. The Byzantines had some cannons of their own, but most of them were useless since the aging walls of Constantinople were not capable of being outfitted with cannons. And in the few attempts that were made, the cannons often backfired, causing more damage to their own structures than to their enemies.

The sultan's bombardment of Constantinople began in earnest in early April. The Ottoman cannons terrorized the populace as their ammunition smashed into the Theodosian Walls of the city. Fortunately for the Byzantines, the massive cannons were extremely unwieldy and difficult for the Turks to reload. The pauses between firing enabled the defenders to quickly repair any breach as best they could.

Over the next several days, the residents became used to the routine of cannonballs smashing into their walls, which was then followed by a quick repair job, with people stuffing wood, stone, and even dirt into the cracks. The sultan's elite troops would try to scale the damaged fortifications only to be assailed with a hail of arrows, stones, or whatever else the Byzantines could throw at them.

The final stage of the siege began that May when Turkish troops began to force their way through the walls of the city. Initially, the Turks were pushed back. In the end, though, the Ottoman forces were just too much to deal with. Upon breaching the walls, they poured into the city. The remaining defenders tried their best to engage the invaders, but the Byzantine emperor was killed in the attempt. It was quite clear to everyone involved that Constantinople was for the taking.

With this prized Byzantine jewel in the Ottoman sultan's cap, Mehmed declared himself not only the sultan of the Ottomans but also styled himself as the emperor of the Romans as well. In truth, the last vestige of the Roman Empire had been eliminated, and as a consequence, almost all of the Balkans would soon be within the Ottomans' grasp.

Chapter 5 – The Balkans as Part of the Ottoman Empire

"Think, when a man or a Prince is tough and strong within, then he can make peace as he pleases; and when he is powerless, a stronger one will come upon him and do whatever he wants with him."

-Vlad III Dracula

The whole Christian world was shocked by the fall of Constantinople in 1453, but for those in the Balkans, the impact was much more immediate. Hungary, in particular, had found itself on the front lines of the Ottoman war machine. With Constantinople extinguished, Hungary was now the Christian vanguard of the Balkans, facing off against either Ottoman troops or the various Balkan forces that had aligned with the Ottomans.

At this time, the Serbian city of Belgrade was a Hungarian possession. And not long after the fall of Constantinople, the sultan turned his eyes toward this metropolis of the Balkans. In 1456, the Ottomans made their way to the Balkan interior to lay siege to Belgrade itself. The Ottomans were riding high, and after their conquest of Constantinople, they must have felt that taking Belgrade would be easy. It was not.

The defenders put up a terrific fight and ended up draining much of the Ottoman Empire's time and resources. It was at this very moment in history that the Son of the Dragon—Vlad Dracula himself—reentered the intrigue of the Balkans in a big way. While Belgrade was under siege, Vlad III met with John Hunyadi in Transylvania and managed to convince Hunyadi to allow him to retake the throne of Wallachia.

In one of the most incredible turnarounds in history, this little-known, orphaned Wallachian prince, who was partially raised by the Ottoman Turks, would come to prove himself as one of the most formidable thorns in the Ottoman sultan's side. Dracula received Hunyadi's blessing that summer of 1456; Hunyadi would perish that August. With the death of the former champion of the Balkans—John Hunyadi—and the rise of a new one—Vlad Dracula—it seemed that the whole Balkan Peninsula was in for a lot of changes.

Nevertheless, if Vlad III Dracula was going to rule, he first had to defeat the current occupant of the Wallachian throne: Vladislav II. As such, Dracula did not pull any punches, and he did not waste any time. The Son of the Dragon gathered his forces and sent them hurtling into Vladislav II's army. The two contingents fought on the Wallachian plains until Dracula and his compatriots were the clear victors of the struggle.

Vladislav II attempted to flee, but he was intercepted and killed. There was now no question who would lead Wallachia, and Vlad III, the Son of the Dragon himself, was placed onto the Wallachian throne. Vlad Dracula was suddenly on the front lines of the Balkan conflict between the Christian powers and the Ottoman Turks. He would somehow have to thread the needle between the two.

On some occasions, Dracula seems to appease the sultan, but on others, he openly defied him. One of the most audacious incidents involving Vlad Dracula occurred in 1461 when he took a small contingent with him to a nearby Turkish base in Giurgiu and tricked them into allowing him access. It has been said that Vlad, who was fluent in Turkish since he was partially raised by the Turks, simply commanded the guards in their native tongues to let him in. The Turks were surprised to hear Turkish commands and obeyed without much question.

But once Vlad Dracula and his band of warriors were allowed in their midst, they turned on their hosts and decimated them. Dracula then fortified this former Turkish citadel and turned it into his own base of operations to launch raids against the Ottomans. Through his own ruthless ingenuity, Dracula would absolutely terrorize the Ottomans. He was rather fond of impaling Turkish soldiers on stakes, which led to the development of another nickname—Vlad the Impaler.

It is said that at one point, in 1462 when Sultan Mehmed II himself led an army to take on Vlad III, he was horrified to find tens of thousands of his own troops impaled on stakes in a gruesome display that spanned several miles along the path to Dracula's domain in Wallachia. As horrendous as some of Vlad Dracula's actions were, there can be no doubt that his ruthless tactics slowed the Ottoman advance down long enough to allow the rest of the Balkans to continue to keep up their resistance to the Ottoman aggression. It is for this reason that many in the Balkans uphold Vlad III as a freedom fighter and folk hero rather than the blood-sucking vampire that Hollywood later made Dracula out to be.

Vlad would ultimately perish in 1476 (some say 1477) while the Ottomans continued their push into the Balkans. This time, the Ottomans were waging war against the Balkan territory of Moldavia. The region was under the authority of a man named Stefan III cel Mare or, as he was otherwise known, "Stephen the Great."

The Ottoman forces had first poured into Stephen's territory in 1475. Just prior to the Ottoman Turks' advance, Stephen had his subjects flee to the mountains while he placed the majority of his army near the village of Vaslui. The Turks were led by Ottoman General

Suleiman Pasha. Stephen sent a contingent of his army out to meet the approaching Turks.

It has been said that Stephen's loyal soldiers put up a fierce fight, but they were greatly outnumbered and soon had to begin their inevitable withdrawal. Even so, they engaged in hit-and-run skirmishes as they made their retreat. Aiding Stephen and his forces were the uneven local terrain and the notoriously rugged roadways. Stephen and the locals knew the best paths to take, but for the Ottomans, who were unfamiliar with the territory, every step was full of treacherous surprises.

This managed to significantly weaken the Ottomans by the time they reached the main Moldavian army at Vaslui. Stephen was then able to unleash the full force of his troops and actually managed to repulse the Turks. This was a great victory for the Moldavians, but even so, they were just buying time. The following year, in 1476, the Turks were back once again with an even larger army.

Stephen knew that there was no way to combat such a large force. Instead of allowing his forces to be rolled over by the Turkish military machine, Stephen burned all the crops in the region and had all who would follow him head for the mountains. The Turks arrived to find nothing but abandoned and burned-out settlements to greet them. This kicked off a guerrilla war, and with the eventual help of the king of Hungary, the Ottomans were eventually forced to retreat.

But even as the Ottoman juggernaut was pulling back in one part of the world, it was almost always advancing in another. In 1479, for example, the Ottomans had reached across the Black Sea all the way to Crimea, which was being administered by a Central Asian tribe called the Tartars. They would ultimately serve as vassals of the Ottomans. The Crimean Khanate, as it would come to be known, would later merge with the Golden Horde, a vestige of the Mongol conquest of Eurasia.

As well as expanding into the Balkans, the Ottomans were also expanding east into Persia and to the southwest, down into Egypt and

Arabia, where they successfully toppled their Islamic neighbors, the Mamluks. This made the Ottoman Empire not just a force to be reckoned with in the Balkans but also the guiding light of Islam, with all other Islamic polities taking notice of this rising star.

The Ottomans were also probing as far west as Italy. The Turks landed in southern Italy in 1480 and seized the city of Otranto. This outpost would come to threaten the entire Italian Peninsula. However, the Turks were basically stuck there, and after Mehmed perished in 1481, they evacuated Oranto and never again threatened the Italians so close to their home.

Mehmed's successor—Bayezid II—would return the focus back to the Balkans and renew the war with Moldavia. After a fierce struggle, Moldavia would finally be brought into the Ottoman fold by the end of the decade, with Stephen the Great admitting defeat in 1485. He had no real choice but to agree to become a vassal of the Ottoman Empire. After the fall of Moldavia, the Ottoman war machine advanced once again toward Hungary. Bayezid II was succeeded by Sultan Selim in 1512, who was, in turn, succeeded by Suleiman I, perhaps better known as Suleiman the Magnificent, in 1520. Suleiman would once again wage war against the Hungarian possession of Belgrade.

Belgrade sat in a very strategic position. It had been a city on the front lines during the Balkan wars between the Turks and Christian European forces. Belgrade rests on the banks of the Danube, and it was seen by the Turks as the gateway for potentially taking the rest of Hungary. As was the case with the Byzantines, the vassal status of Hungary was not enough to ward off invasion. The sultan himself accompanied the military campaign to lay siege to Belgrade.

It took some time, but Belgrade fell into Ottoman hands in 1521. Belgrade was then used as a forward launching base into the rest of Europe, just as Suleiman had planned. Hungary's ruler—King Louis II—just like Stephen the Great before him, tried his best to stall the Turkish advance. Interestingly, King Louis II also had a commander named Stephen. And it was the enigmatic yet incredible Stephen Bathory who would lead the offensive against the Turks.

As an interesting aside, Stephen Bathory's granddaughter— Elizabeth Bathory—was the infamous "Blood Countess." Providing even further fodder for vampiric Balkan lore, it has been said that Countess Elizabeth Bathory liked to have people killed so she could bathe in their blood. Both Vlad the Impaler and the Blood Countess do indeed paint a rather blood-curdling image of the Balkans. Of course, there is much more to the Balkans than their legendary tales and exploits.

At any rate, it was Elizabeth's granddad Stephen who would do battle with the Turks at the epic Battle of Mohacs in 1526. The Ottomans came loaded with heavy artillery, cavalry, and some fifteen thousand fanatically loyal crack troops called the Janissaries. The Hungarians had some big guns of their own, and the battle commenced with the firing of their cannons.

This was then immediately followed by a charge of Hungarian cavalry. The cavalry was highly effective, and these units were able to drive deep into the enemy ranks. So deep, in fact, that at one point, it seemed that they were going to make contact with the sultan himself. But before any such thing could occur, Turkish heavy artillery, which had been placed in a solid line, opened up on the Hungarian horsemen and broke their charge.

The Hungarians were sent rushing back in retreat, and they were then horrified to realize that they had been outflanked. Their base camp was already being overrun. They saw Turkish troops indiscriminately kill civilians at their camp. The whole Hungarian army then began to retreat. In their panicked withdrawal, King Louis perished. He did not die at the hands of an enemy; his horse lost its footing and came crashing down on top of him.

With the Hungarian army defeated and on the run, the Turks seized the nearby town of Buda. After cutting a path through Hungary, the Ottomans would end up threatening the European heartland—most notably Vienna, Austria—which was first besieged by Ottoman troops in 1529. The Ottomans found the Viennese ready for them, however. After facing off against well-armed and disciplined troops in the middle of a snowstorm, the Turks had had enough.

They ended up retreating back to their holdings in Hungary. The Ottomans would make another attempt in 1532. It, too, would fail. The sultan would end up signing a peace treaty with the Habsburg ruler of Austria, Holy Emperor Ferdinand I (he was also the archduke of Austria). However, by 1537, battles in the disputed regions between Austria and Turkish-controlled Hungary erupted again. The Austrian forces engaged the Ottoman army in the Croatian region of Valpovo, only to face a terrible defeat. This defeat was followed by an even more decisive one in 1541, in which the Austrian army was annihilated at the Austrian-controlled city of Pest.

In the meantime, the Turkish troops in Buda decided to go ahead and annex their Hungarian vassals outright. By 1543, almost all of Hungary was under Ottoman occupation, with only a very small borderland region of Austria/Hungary left. It was an entirely meager and ineffective buffer between the Ottomans and the Habsburg Austrians.

Major moves by the Ottomans were once again being made by 1595 under Sultan Mehmed III. It was around this time that Mehmed was alerted to the fact that his current puppet ruler of Transylvania, Sigismund Bathory, had just switched sides on him. As we have seen, both Transylvania and Wallachia, two Balkan principalities on the front lines of the struggle between Christian Europe and the Ottoman Turks, had often switched their allegiances back and forth whenever it was deemed expedient to do so.

This time around, Transylvania had decided to help out the Austrians. This led to Mehmed III launching an assault that would take his forces up to Bucharest, although they would be repulsed. The Austrians then capitalized on these gains by seizing several important Ottoman outposts in northern Hungary. As great as these gains were for Austria and Hungary, the Austro-Hungarians were soon in for a major defeat. For it was shortly thereafter, in the fall of 1596, that an allied force led by Archduke Maximillian of Austria and Sigismund Bathory of Transylvania attempted to deal a fatal blow to the Turks in the Balkans.

On October 24th, they launched an attack on Ottoman positions in eastern Hungary near the village of Keresztes. The Turks were pushed back, and a couple of days later, the Austro-Hungarians launched another assault. The Austrian and Hungarian forces were once again successful in tearing into the Ottoman lines and pushing the Turks back. Even so, the cautious archduke urged restraint, telling his men not to pursue the Turks past the Danube. However, the overzealous troops refused to listen, and after forcing the Turks to flee, they pursued.

Even worse, once they stumbled upon the Turks' abandoned encampment, many of the troops apparently forgot all about the war they were fighting and focused on plundering the camp instead. The Turks had left many valuable possessions behind in their hasty retreat, and Austrian and Hungarian knights, dispensing with all notions of chivalry, were getting off their horses to gather up the loot.

While a large part of the Austro-Hungarian army was dismounted and distracted by their plunder, the Ottomans rallied and launched a massive counterattack against them. The Austro-Hungarians barely had time to get back on their horses to lead a disorderly and chaotic retreat. During their flight, thousands perished, and even worse, some of the best Austrian artillery had to be abandoned, which went directly into the hands of the Turks. A battle that initially seemed to be the Austro-Hungarians to win devolved into a miserable failure. This would put them on the defensive, and much of their gains would be lost as the Ottomans continued to consolidate their hold on the Balkans.

By the early 1680s, the situation had become even more dire, as the Ottomans launched themselves out of the Balkans and into

Austria itself. In 1683, the Ottomans would once again instigate an assault on the Austrian capital of Vienna. An Ottoman force of about 100,000 men was said to have stood at the gates of Vienna. The inhabitants, who were tasked with defending their city, were just a fraction of that size.

As such, there was no chance of open combat between the defenders and the aggressors since the numerically superior Ottomans would have made short work of them in open warfare. Thus, the Austrians holed themselves inside their fortifications and hoped for a miracle. The Turks incessantly chipped away at the city walls of Vienna, eager to make a breach so that the full force of their army could storm inside.

But the city's fortifications were indeed built well, and it was clear that it would take some time to tear them down. During this struggle, the Turks sent miners under the walls to plant bombs that would cause the foundations to be ripped asunder. However, the Austrians were quite good at intercepting the miners. The inhabitants of the city would kill them and neutralize their bombs, ensuring their safety.

The defenders of Vienna relentlessly countered every effort of the Turks they could, but they would not be able to keep up this pace forever. If no help from the outside arrived, Vienna likely would have eventually been overrun, much like Constantinople had two centuries prior.

Fortunately for Vienna, help was indeed on the way. Right when the city of Vienna seemed on the verge of falling, a force of Polish knights came racing forth from the west. Yes, in its darkest hour, Austria's "knights in shining armor" had arrived. This contingent was led by Poland's potentate, John Sobieski III. This man would go down as the veritable savior of western Europe.

King Sobieski and his famous Winged Hussars were able to alter the course of history by pushing back the Turks, who had arrived from the Balkans. The Winged Hussars were also assisted by a small contingent of Teutonic Knights, and this combined force was able to tear right through the Ottoman lines. Making matters worse for the Turks was the sultan's belligerent insistence on making the Ottomans' primary focus the gates of Vienna, even though the rear flanks of the Ottoman army were being decimated.

Apparently, the sultan felt that if he could just tear down Vienna's gates and send his troops inside, the war would be won. But the gates held, and the Turks essentially found themselves banging their heads against a wall while the Winged Hussars and Teutonic Knights tore into their backs. After a large number of his men had been cut down, the sultan finally called off the siege and directed his army to retreat back to the Balkans.

This dramatic retreat has often been marked by historians as the beginning of the Ottoman decline. The deterioration of the Ottoman Empire was then all but sealed in 1699 at the Battle of Zenta, in which the Turks were forced to cede Transylvania and almost all of Hungary to Austria. The Turkish menace of the Balkans had indeed been decisively pushed back.

And for much of the rest of its history, the Ottoman Empire would be primarily on the defensive, focused on holding onto the territory it already had rather than gaining more. Soon, it would be all the Ottomans could do to hold onto and consolidate their holdings as formerly subjugated people—especially in the Balkans—began to openly fight for their freedom.

Chapter 6 – The Balkan Wars of Independence

"I will always fight for peace. But unfortunately, it is war that drives us forward. It is war that makes the major turns. It makes Wall Street function. It makes all the bastards in the Balkans function."

-Emir Kusturica

The Ottomans would spend much of the 18th century struggling to hold onto or alternately struggling to regain territory in the Balkans. In 1702, the Ottomans lost some territories to Russia but were able to regain them, albeit not without a struggle, in 1711. They also lost Morea to the Venetians, but in 1715, the Ottomans were able to reclaim that piece of the Balkan puzzle as well. But no matter what they tried, nothing could prevent them from losing their Balkan crown jewel of Belgrade, which was pried out of the Ottoman Empire's grip by the Habsburgs in 1717.

Nevertheless, the Ottoman forces would rally. By 1739, with the Treaty of Belgrade, this Balkan metropolis would be back in the Ottoman orbit. But even while outside powers, such as the Austrians and the Ottomans, were deciding the fate of the Balkans, the people of Belgrade were certainly getting sick and tired of this seemingly never-ending tug of war. Due to the ongoing conflict, many migrated out of Belgrade altogether, heading to less tumultuous territory under Austrian control.

Just prior to Belgrade returning to the Ottomans, in 1737, many native Serbs had sided with the Austrian forces and openly rebelled against their Ottoman overlords. Rather than face the wrath of the Ottomans, many Serbs migrated north to Habsburg territory after Belgrade was regained by the Ottoman Empire. This migration was almost of biblical proportions, with the Serbian Patriarch Arsenije Jovanovic IV, like some Balkan version of Moses, leading his people out of harm's way.

The local citizens of the Balkans were not the only ones who rebelled during this period. The sultan's elite force, the Janissaries, also began to frequently cause the sultan trouble closer to home. The Janissaries were mostly made up of young men who had been taken from Christian families in the Balkans through the devshirme, which really was nothing more than a child tax.

It is absolutely abhorrent to consider it today, but a major part of the Ottoman war machine was the requirement that had been placed upon subject people to sacrifice one of their own children to the Ottoman state. Snatched from their families, these little boys were indoctrinated and trained as elite soldiers for the Ottoman Empire. It was the peculiar nature of how the Janissaries were brought up that made them such a ruthless and effective fighting force.

Essentially raised by the Ottoman state, they were brainwashed with Ottoman propaganda from their youth. Most were taken before they could form lasting memories with their family, so they knew nothing but the cult-like atmosphere that they were brought up in. With no family or any other ties to hold them down, they would develop a fanatical loyalty to the sultan and the Ottoman Empire.

However, after repeated military failures, these kidnapped men of the Balkans began to rise up and rebel against their Ottoman masters. In fact, the situation became so bad that the Ottoman administration ended up putting more weight behind local militias in the Balkans rather than putting all of their faith in the Janissary corps. These local militias were called *martolos*, and they were tasked with protecting the Balkan frontier.

The *martolos* were fairly successful in their role as Balkan border guards, but in time, they would become disenchanted with the Ottoman regime. And it would be the very Balkan militias the Ottomans had established to keep the peace that would end up lending aid to uprisings by the Balkan citizens. The use of these provincial militias also had the effect of weakening centralized control over the Ottoman Empire.

Such a situation would be similar to the United States disbanding its federal troops in favor of relying primarily on state-run National Guard units. Such an arrangement could prove adequate in protecting territory, but at the same time, it would diminish centralized control. It could also lead to differences in how states conducted themselves and even facilitate breakaway republics. And this scenario is indeed what began to transpire within the Ottoman Empire.

As the Balkan militias grew more powerful, they were able to throw around more and more weight as it pertained to how the Balkan territories were being administered. Soon, even though the provinces recognized the sultan on an official level, it was becoming clear that they were employing growing levels of autonomy. And as they grew stronger, the central figure of the sultan grew increasingly weaker.

This was in large part due to a change in Ottoman policy that required the sultan's prospective heirs to be essentially isolated from the world. Known as the "cage policy," this was developed in order to prevent infighting and a crisis of succession upon the death of a sultan. The sultan's sons were largely confined to the palace, and their only real interactions were with their parents, tutors, and women from the harem. This isolation prevented the sons of the sultan from developing powerful factions with which they could wage war against each other upon their father's death.

But while it was successful in preventing infighting among the sultan's sons during the transition of power, it also had the effect of making the new sultan incredibly inept when it came to governing. One can only imagine what it must have been like to have a person completely isolated from the world suddenly thrust upon the throne of one of the world's largest empires. In reality, the cage policy essentially ensured that the sultan would be largely a pawn of his administrators, who would be the real power behind the throne.

Incredibly corrupt and non-beneficial policies began to be orchestrated right under the sultan's nose. Rather than taking measures to improve the Ottoman Empire, many corrupt officials sought to enrich themselves and the loyal factions that supported them. This led to unfair laws being passed, as well as exorbitant taxation. Those who came out on the wrong end of this corrupt legislation often fled to the Balkan frontier to get away from it.

Oftentimes, in the Balkans, these jaded members of Ottoman bureaucracy would set down roots and create their own powerful factions on the Ottoman periphery. This, of course, caused only more instability and led to even more opportunities for eruptions of internecine violence in the Balkans.

By the year 1800, the life of the average Balkan resident was fairly miserable. They were subject to high taxes and lorded over by local strongmen. Pressed and afflicted on all sides, it should not be too surprising to learn that the locals began to rebel. One of the most notable of these rebellions was the First Serbian Uprising, which erupted in the Balkans in February of 1804. The seeds for this uprising were first planted when Ottoman Janissaries revolted against their own vizier—Hadzi Mustafa Pasha—killing him in 1801 and then attempting to administer a chunk of the Balkans on their own.

Some might have actually viewed the Janissaries as liberators, but they proved to be even harsher than either the Ottoman sultan or the assassinated grand vizier. In the Balkan enclave that they had seized, the Janissaries were absolutely tyrannical. They taxed the life out of the peasants and took away all the rights and privileges that the Ottoman authorities had previously given them. The Janissaries also virtually enslaved the people, forcing them to do manual labor.

Outraged, some local Serbian leaders sent word to the sultan of what was happening, hoping to get some relief. After the Janissaries heard of this request for assistance, they decided to take out reprisals on the Serbs. And in January of 1804, this culminated in the mass murder of the Serbian elite. The Janissaries conducted systematic executions in what went down as the "Slaughter of the Knezes." The Serbian leaders who were massacred then had their heads placed on stakes so that they would serve as an example to others thinking of rebelling.

However, rather than having the people fall in line, the incident had the opposite effect. Entire Serbian families fled into the wilderness, where a full-scale resistance was mounted. The situation was particularly galling to Serbian Christians, who had long been paying taxes to the sultan for his "protection." Christians all over the Ottoman Empire were forced to pay the jizya, a tax that allowed them to follow their faith in peace. Although they were seen as second-class citizens, as long as they paid the tax, they were supposed to be protected from physical violence.

With town leaders' heads staring at them from stakes, it did not take much for the locals to wonder just what they were being taxed for if the Ottoman government could no longer protect them from its own Janissaries. Realizing that they had to take matters into their own hands, the local Serbs mounted a vicious form of guerrilla warfare against their oppressors—the tyrannical Janissary elite.

On February 14th, 1804, the leading figures of this Serbian uprising met at the town of Orasac to plot the course of what would become nothing short of a revolution. It was here that they actually held an assembly and, with a simple show of hands, democratically elected the man they would choose to be their leader—Djordje Petrovic (Đorđe Petrović).

Petrovic was a simple cattle merchant, but his selfless character was trusted by the group. He also had previous military experience, having served in the local militia in the past. His knowledge of the battlefield would indeed prove invaluable, and under Petrovic's leadership, the Serbs soon had the Janissaries on the run. In a very short period of time, they had reclaimed much of their territory, and the Janissaries themselves ended up largely confined to their forts.

The Janissaries apparently realized that they had bitten off a little more than they could chew, and they actually reached out to the Austrian Habsburgs for help. They did not ask for military aid since they knew there was no way the Austrians would side with them against the Serbs. However, they knew that due to the political intrigue of the Balkans, there was a chance that the Austrians would be interested in helping to at least broker a peaceful settlement.

Such a thing would have allowed the Janissaries to avoid bringing down the sultan's wrath upon them and allow them to save them some face. After all, a peaceful settlement would allow them to make their exit from the volatile situation they had created. The Austrians did facilitate a meeting in the border town of Zemun, which was in close proximity to Belgrade, in which the Serbs and Janissary officials met face to face. But the meeting did not produce any results.

Initially, the Serbs were merely fighting to overthrow the tyrannical Janissaries and restore traditional Ottoman rule. But they were now leaning more and more toward fighting for their complete independence. These sentiments were encouraged both by the Austrians as well as the Russians. The Serbs sought assistance from the Russians, but the Russians were already bogged down fighting the French in the Napoleonic Wars that had erupted. They were not in a position to lend direct military support. However, they did supply weapons and boosted morale by offering to back an independent Serbian state in the Balkans on a diplomatic front.

When the sultan got word of these events, he turned on the rebels. And what was a local skirmish between two competing provincial authorities became an outright insurrection in the eyes of the Ottoman state. As such, the sultan sent troops to put down the rebellion.

You might think that the prospect of the Ottoman juggernaut marching against them would give these rebels pause—but it did not. They gathered their arms and faced off against the Ottoman regular army at the Battle of Ivankovac in 1805. Against all odds, they were successful in repulsing the Turks. That November, the Serbian rebels then scored another victory when they seized the fort of Smederevo. They subsequently made it the headquarters of their rebellion. The Serbs were no longer just a roving band of revolutionaries in the wilderness; they had established a formidable army of their own.

The next major phase of the revolution occurred in 1806 when the Serbian forces put down yet another Ottoman regiment at the Battle of Misar. The greatest accomplishment of all, however, happened that December when the Serbs managed to seize control of Belgrade.

At this point, the Serbs had the upper hand and were in an advantageous position for possible negotiations. They sent a representative off to Constantinople (today's Istanbul) to enter into negotiations with the sultan. The sultan did come around to some of the Serbs' demands, but as far as the rebels were concerned, he did not go far enough, so the hostilities continued.

In the meantime, the Ottoman Empire was becoming increasingly unstable. Sultan Selim III was assassinated in 1808, and he was replaced by Mustafa IV. However, Mustafa IV would not be on the throne for long, as he was supplanted by Sultan Mahmud II. The following year, war erupted between Russia and the Ottoman Empire. For the Serbs, of course, this appeared to be the opportunity they were waiting for—the big brother of the Balkans appeared ready to help them achieve a stunning victory.

But cooperation between the Russians and the Serbs was not always ideal, and despite previous victories, the Serbian forces faced a devastating defeat at the hands of the Ottomans at the Battle of Cegar.

It was named after Cegar Hill, which was located in the middle of two villages—Kamenica and Donji Matejevac—where much of the fighting took place. The initial objective of the Serbs was to take the nearby fortress of Nis. However, the defenders held out, as the Serbs lacked strong artillery. They were unable to force their way into the compound.

Ottoman reinforcements arrived in the tens of thousands, and the Serbian revolutionaries were soon surrounded on all sides. The Serbs were systematically cut down until they reached the point of no return. Rather than surrender, the Serbian commander, Stevan Sindelic, actually detonated a huge stockpile of gunpowder just as the Turks were closing in, resulting in a massive explosion that killed him, his comrades, and several Ottoman soldiers.

After the Serbs were defeated, the Ottoman commander, Hurshid Pasha, actually had a large stone tower constructed in which Serbian skulls were inserted into the masonry. Known as "Skull Tower," the structure still stands today, with hundreds of Serbian skulls staring out from each side; there are fourteen rows of skulls from top to bottom. This dreadful tower was erected to frighten the rest of the Serbs into submission, but modern-day Serbs have upheld the grisly site not as a place of foreboding but as a national symbol of resistance to the Ottoman oppressors.

Indeed, in 1833, a visiting writer from France, Alphonse de Lamartine, shared that very sentiment. And he perhaps described it best when, upon encountering Skull Tower, he declared, "My eyes and my heart greeted the remains of those brave men whose cut-off heads made the cornerstone of the independence of their homeland. May the Serbs keep this monument! It will always teach their children the value of the independence of a people, showing them the real price their fathers had to pay for it." The site has since been opened up to the public, and it is now even considered something of a tourist attraction, despite its grisly past.

Sadly enough, however, the situation for the Serbs at the time of the uprising would only go from bad to worse. Russia faced a renewed threat from France, so it abandoned the Serbs when they needed its forces and aid the most. By 1813, the Ottomans had ended up seizing most of what the rebels had gained.

After the uprising was put down, vengeful massacres ensued, and a flood of refugees left their homeland, primarily for Austrian- or Russian-controlled territory. But no matter how much terror the Ottomans inflicted, they could not keep down the Serbian populace for good. In 1815, yet another popular uprising took place. This time around, the Serbs were able to shake off the Ottomans for good, and their independence as a sovereign nation was finally recognized in 1830.

While the Serbs engaged in their final struggle for independence, their Balkan cousins, the Greeks, began to grow restless against their Ottoman taskmasters. The Greek War of Independence first broke out in 1821. There were revolts and uprisings for some time, but it was only when Greek freedom fighter Theodoros Kolokotronis and his forces successfully took over the Ottoman administrative outpost of Tripolitsa that things really began to heat up.

Infuriated at the success of the revolt, the sultan of the Ottoman Empire decided to engage in collective punishment. He actually rounded up the patriarch of the Greek Orthodox Church and had him executed. The patriarch had nothing to do with the revolt; he had actually called for peace. However, he was a symbol of Greek culture and faith, so the sultan decided to take his wrath out on him anyhow. The killing of the patriarch was followed by a general massacre of Greeks all throughout the Ottoman Empire.

Such things present an uncomfortable truth for many Turks today, but denying history does not change what actually happened. And there was indeed a wholesale slaughter of Greeks that took place in reprisal for the revolutionary gains that were made on the Greek mainland. Despite all of the bloodshed, the Greek freedom fighters of the Balkans soldiered on, and in 1822, they actually forged their own constitution.

In the meantime, popular support for the Greeks began to grow abroad. Even though foreign governments of the west were slow to cast in their lot with the Greeks, many prominent individual citizens began to demand that they do so. Among them was the British writer Lord Byron. Byron actually went to Greece to fight with the rebels, and he would die in Greece in 1824.

The outcry to support Greece soon became so great that Britain, France, and Russia could no longer resist. In 1827, all three signed the Treaty of London, which stated that they recognized Greek independence from the Ottoman Empire. But although recognition was made, the war still had to be won. Greece's allies, which were now drawn into the conflict, managed to hand the Ottomans a decisive defeat that very year when they bombarded an Ottoman armada at Navarino Bay. The Ottoman ships were sunk, and with it, so, too, was any hope of the Ottoman Empire reclaiming its Balkan holdings of Greece.

The Russians, in the meantime, had ventured deep into the Balkan interior and managed to seize Edirne (Adrianople) in 1829. This resulted in the Ottomans recognizing Serbian independence in 1830. The terms of Greek independence were finally settled soon after in 1833. The Greeks had been dreaming of an independent state since the fall of Constantinople in 1453, and now their freedom had finally arrived.

The next major move for independence in the Balkans would occur in Bulgaria. In the spring of 1876, the April Uprising took place. The Bulgarians rose up against the Ottomans only to be brutally suppressed. It is said that tens of thousands of Bulgarians were killed in the process. This bloodshed led to a loud outcry in both western Europe, Russia, and the United States. The leading powers held the Constantinople Conference, in which certain demands were once again placed upon the Ottoman government.

When the Ottomans refused these demands, the Russians realized they had a pretext to launch an assault on the Ottoman Empire. Russia, with the assistance of Bulgarian insurgents, began waging war against the Ottomans in 1877. The war went well enough for the Russians, and by the following year, they had fought their way through the Balkans all the way to the very doorstep of Constantinople.

The British, however, preferred to have the Ottoman Empire as a buffer between an expansionist Russia and their own interests in the eastern Mediterranean. They could not allow the Ottomans to be overrun by the Russians. Preferring to keep some semblance of the status quo, the British convinced their Russian counterparts to come to the diplomatic table instead. The ensuing peace talks set the foundation for a free Bulgaria. They also ensured independence for Serbia, Romania, and Montenegro.

Bulgaria itself was more of a work in progress, with the northern reaches of this Balkan state becoming sovereign while the south remained as an Ottoman domain. Almost as an afterthought, the treaty handed Bosnia and Herzegovina to the Austro-Hungarians (Austria-Hungary was officially formed in 1867).

As minor as this might have seemed at the time, this decision would have big implications since it was in a disenchanted Bosnia and Herzegovina that ultra-nationalist forces would come to prominence. And it was in this fermenting backdrop of nationalism that a Serbian assassin would kill an Austrian archduke and ignite the terrible conflagration that would become known as the First World War.

Chapter 7 – The Balkans and the World Wars

"My people are going to learn the principles of democracy, the dictates of truth and the teachings of science. Superstition must go."

-Mustafa Kemal Ataturk

Just prior to the outbreak of the First World War, the Balkans, in general, were becoming an increasingly tumultuous place. The reason behind this tumult was largely due to the unfinished business of borders and strategic alliances. The Great Powers had aided the Balkan people by freeing them from Ottoman dominion, yet they were also to blame for carving up unreliable borders for the Balkan states. They also had their own self-interests, which invited corrupt dealings and encouraged Balkan leaders to play one Great Power against another.

It was clear the Balkans were a powder keg by 1912 with the eruption of the so-called "Balkan Wars." The wars began after Greece, Montenegro, Serbia, and Bulgaria formed the Balkan League and began to voice their concerns over the status of their nationals who still resided in certain sections of the Ottoman Empire. Even though the Great Powers had drawn up lines to create new borders for these countries, several of their countrymen had found themselves caught behind Ottoman lines.

The Balkan League came together and voiced its concern for what it perceived to be the mistreatment of these various Balkan peoples at the hands of the Ottomans. The league issued a series of demands to the Ottoman Empire, and once these demands were rejected, the league declared war. The Bulgarians launched an offensive into eastern Thrace and ended up at the gates of Constantinople, much like the Russians had done just a few decades prior. However, the Turks were able to hold their own around the so-called "Catalca line" of defenses, as well as on the Gallipoli Peninsula.

In the meantime, the Serbs launched attacks on Skopje and Monastir before fighting through Albania and seizing Kosovo. They then joined forces with the army from Montenegro, which was already in the region.

While this was going on, the Greek troops hit Thessaly and then launched an assault on Macedonia. The Greeks ended up repatriating Thessaloniki back into the Greek fold after the Ottoman garrison there surrendered on November 8th, 1912.

The Bulgarians actually wished to seize Thessaloniki for themselves, and when Bulgarian troops arrived on the scene the following day, they were actually dismayed that the Greeks had beaten them to it. Comically enough, the former Ottoman administrator of the city, Tahsin Pasha, is said to have told the disappointed Bulgarians, "I have only one Thessaloniki, which I have surrendered."

The Bulgarian and Serbian forces went on to seize Adrianople, and the Greek troops poured into Ioannina, delivering a decisive blow to the Ottoman army at the Battle of Bizani. Soon after this, the forces from Montenegro managed to seize the Ottoman outpost of Shkoder. The Ottoman Empire was unable to continue the war, and it finally sued for peace. This resulted in the implementation of a new round of agreements, which were set forth in a new Treaty of London in 1913.

The agreement allowed Greece to take just about every island in the Aegean Sea, and it was awarded all its former land west of the so-called "Enos-Midia" line to the Balkan League. But in reality, the treaty left more questions than answers. Soon, new territorial disputes emerged, which would result in the Second Balkan War in the summer of 1913. This war was different from the first because it saw Balkan League members actually fighting each other.

Bulgaria, in particular, was incensed that the Serbs and Greeks had seized portions of Macedonia. The war began with Bulgaria battling it out with the former Balkan League members of Serbia and Greece. Things really heated up when Montenegro sided with the Ottoman Empire to take on Bulgaria. Romania then entered the picture, crossing over Bulgaria's northern borders to engage in hostilities. In essence, what had erupted among all of these combatants was akin to a mini-world war in the Balkans.

The war did not go well for Bulgaria, and a joint Serbian/Greek force was able to knock the Bulgarians back across Bulgaria's southern borders. While this was happening, the Romanians were entering Bulgaria from the north. After everything was said and done, rather than gaining land, Bulgaria was forced to give up even more land to Serbia, Greece, and Romania. Even the Ottoman Empire benefited since it was agreed that Bulgaria would hand back eastern Thrace, as well as Adrianople, to the Ottomans.

Interestingly, both the Austro-Hungarians and the Ottomans were becoming very wary of the Balkan countries, and they found it in their mutual interest to have a say in what occurred in the Balkan states. This state of affairs set the stage for the eventual alignment of the Central Powers during World War One, in which—beyond all odds—the Austro-Hungarians would actually fight alongside their old enemy, the Ottomans.

It was, of course, the assassination of Austrian Archduke Franz Ferdinand that would spark the global conflict. Ferdinand was visiting Bosnia and Herzegovina when he was gunned down by a Serbian nationalist. It was said that the assassin—Gavrilo Princip—was linked to a Serbian militant group called the Black Hand, which was said to have been organized by none other than the Serbian army. It was these supposed connections that led Austria-Hungary to hold the Serbian government responsible for what had happened.

The Austro-Hungarians then issued a series of demands against Serbia itself. The demands were draconian in the extreme, and their implementation would have threatened Serbia's very sovereignty. The Austro-Hungarians ultimately knew that the demands would be rejected, and they would go on to use Serbia's refusal as a pretext for war. And sure enough, when Serbia refused to meet all of these harsh demands, war was declared.

But due to the nature of alliances in those days, a war declared on one quickly developed into a war declared on all. Germany and the Ottoman Empire sided with Austria-Hungary, while Britain, France, and Russia sided with Serbia. World War One had begun. And what about the other Balkan nations? On which side did they fall? Of all the Balkan states, only the most disgruntled nation from the previous conflicts, Bulgaria, openly sided with the Central Powers of Austria-Hungary, Germany, and the Ottoman Empire. Serbia, Montenegro, Greece, and even Albania all fought on the Allied side.

Since the Ottomans were widely viewed as the weakest member of the Central Powers, the Allies focused on toppling them early on. The British and Australians launched a major offensive against the Ottoman Empire in April of 1915, in which they attempted a landing on the Gallipoli Peninsula. However, the Ottoman resistance was much stiffer than anticipated, and the Ottoman troops were able to beat the British advance back to the beaches.

The British would remain virtually trapped on the shores, and for the next several months, they were hit with relentless heavy fire. The operation actually had to be called off, and the Allied soldiers departed in January of 1916, having to admit defeat—at least as it pertained to the ill-fated Gallipoli campaign.

It was right around this time that the Austro-Hungarian, German, and Bulgarian forces assailed the Serbian positions, forcing the Serbs to flee to southwest Albania. The British and French forces tried to back the Serbs up but were, in turn, sent on their heels against a resurgent Bulgarian force. The Serbs ended up fleeing all the way to the Albanian Alps, where they were constantly harassed by Albanian fighters. It is said that the fleeing Serbs suffered around 100,000 casualties, and by the time they managed to reach the Adriatic Sea and secure evacuation on French and British freighters, their numbers had been reduced to just 70,000.

Shortly thereafter, Montenegro was knocked out of the war, as it was seized by Austria-Hungary. As if the complexities of the Balkans were not enough, it is worth noting how Austria and Hungary had essentially become one. It was defined as such ever since the Compromise of 1867. It is for this reason that rather than mentioning the Austrian Empire, we refer to the "dual monarchy" of the Balkans, known as the Austro-Hungarian Empire.

At any rate, the Bulgarians, in these early stages of World War One, were pushing deep into Macedonia and making demands for a greater Bulgaria. The Allied forces would rebound in November of 1916 and push the Bulgarians back to the Macedonian town of Bitola.

It was around this time that Romanian forces surged into Transylvania in an attempt to seize the territory. However, they were easily repulsed however by the Austro-Hungarian and German forces. The Bulgarians then linked up with the Austro-Hungarians and Germans, and this united force was able to push the Romanians all the way back to Moldavia, leaving hundreds of thousands of their own dead behind in the process.

During these events, Russia was going from bad to worse. The Russian troops appeared ill-equipped and ill-prepared, and the civil unrest in Russia itself had reached a boiling point. Things were so bad that the Russian leader, Tsar Nicholas II, was actually forced to abdicate in March 1917.

Russian revolutionaries took over the government and sent the Russian nation down a path that would lead to the reformation of Russia, transforming it into the communist Soviet Union. The founders of the Soviet Union had no desire to continue the war that the tsar had started, so they sued for peace as soon as possible. And with the signing of the Treaty of Brest-Litovsk in March of 1918, Russia was officially out of the war. The former tsar, Nicholas II, and his family were killed that July.

Romania was heavily dependent on Russia, and as such, Romania officially withdrew shortly after Russia. Romania was forced to sign the Treaty of Bucharest, in which it ceded land to Bulgaria and became occupied by Germany. As bad as things seemed for the remaining Allied powers, they would soon drastically improve—not so much on the Balkan front but rather on the Western Front.

While engaging in the battles in the Balkans, the British and French had been locked into a bloody stalemate of trench warfare with the Germans in western Europe. The entrance of the United States into the war on the side of the Allies in late 1917 would ultimately tilt the war in the Allies' favor. With their forces in a better position on the Western Front, the Allies were free to focus more on the Balkans. They delivered a decisive blow to Bulgarian troops stationed in Macedonia. The Bulgarians were unable to recover and sued for peace.

The first sign that the Central Powers were cracking under the pressure was the surrender of Bulgaria, with their armistice being signed on September 29th, 1918. Shortly thereafter, a battered and weary Ottoman Empire also signed an armistice on October 30th. This was then followed by the initial antagonist of this struggle—Austria-Hungary—signing its own armistice on November 3rd. Germany was suddenly the last Central Power standing, and it, too, would ultimately sue for peace on November 11th, 1918. This last and final armistice effectively ended the terrible conflagration that came to be known as World War One.

In the aftermath of this terrible war, the Balkan question would once again come to the forefront. What should the world do with all of these warring Balkan nations? It was in the confusion of rebuilding the post-war Balkans that the Balkanized conglomeration of Yugoslavia came into being. Out of the ashes of two empires—the Austro-Hungarian and the Ottoman Empires—this super Balkan state came about by merging Serbia, Croatia, and Slovenia together.

Greece was awarded western Thrace, as well as portions of western Anatolia. Greece wanted more for its efforts, though, and it was willing to continue fighting in order to get it.

Certain segments of the Ottoman Empire were appalled at this latest loss of territory. Mustafa Kemal Ataturk (better known simply as Ataturk), who was riding high on this outrage, called for the nationalization of Turkey and the dismantling of the Ottoman Empire.

Greek nationalists worried about losing their previous gains, and they appealed to the British for help. However, the British were tired of war, and they were not willing to render Greece any further aid. So, the Greeks decided to take matters into their own hands. On March 23rd, 1921, they launched a unilateral attack against the newly christened state of Turkey. But the Greeks were quickly knocked back by the Turks. As they attempted to make a retreat, they were harried by both Turkish troops and enraged Turkish nationals. The situation became just about intolerable.

Even if the Greeks managed to defeat the Turkish troops, the hostility of the locals would make it untenable. Yet, if the Greek army was to pull out, an even worse fate would have been in store for the local Greek residents since they would then, no doubt, be subject to reprisals. And the Greek leadership, which feared as much, was proven to be absolutely right. After the Greeks troops were defeated and forced to retreat in the fall of 1922, Turkish troops carried out a systematic massacre of the Greek residents of Smyrna. The Greek sections of the city were set ablaze. It has been said that 25,000 died and that 200,000 were left homeless.

The Greeks were forced to sign the Treaty of Lausanne with Turkey. Despite their military loss, the treaty was fairly lenient on the Greeks, as it allowed them to keep much of their pre-World War I territory. However, they did have to give up all territory in Anatolia itself. This roughly created the boundaries of the modern-day Greek state, as well as the modern boundaries of Turkey.

The most momentous of these developments occurred shortly after when a "population exchange" between the former combatants took place. In 1923, Greece and Turkey basically swapped their Greek and Turkish populations. Thus, the Greeks in Anatolia headed for Greece, while the Turks in mainland Greece headed for Anatolia. These are fairly drastic measures, but in light of all the abuses and atrocities that had been committed against civilians, it was viewed as the only real way to keep the peace at the time. About 100,000 or so Greeks chose to stay in Constantinople (today's Istanbul; the name change would come about in 1930).

Due to the collapse of both the Austro-Hungarian and the Ottoman Empires after the war, Germany had to pay the vast bulk of the reparations. It was these reparations, as well as the unrealistic boundaries forced upon the Balkans, which were both dictated by the Treaty of Versailles, that would ultimately sow the seeds for World War Two. By the late 1930s, Germany would form the Axis alliance with Italy and Japan. Although Italy and Japan both fought on the "winning" side of World War One, both countries felt slighted at the war's end, as they had received very little for their efforts. It was under the guise of all-out fascism that these countries would attempt to right their perceived wrongs.

The Great Depression, which occurred in the 1930s, had made the Balkans and the world even more unstable, and the Balkan nations began looking for trade partners. Many of these Balkan states would look to the Axis for aid. For example, Italy dominated Albanian trade, and Germany would come to dominate much of the rest.

World War Two began in Europe when Germany invaded Poland in the fall of 1939, but it can be said to have begun in the Balkans when Italy occupied Albania in April 1939. From Albania, the Italians would launch an offensive into Greece on October 28th, 1940. However, this push into Greece was met with considerable resistance, and the Italians were repulsed. The Italians tried again in the spring of 1941, but they were beaten back a second time.

Germany, which was aided by Bulgaria, had rolled into Yugoslavia, successfully seizing the territory in April of 1941. The Germans then invaded Greece from both the north and the south, dealing it a decisive defeat. With Greece under Axis control, Yugoslavia was dissolved. Chunks of Yugoslavia were divvied up between Germany, Italy, Hungary, and Bulgaria. The rest was fashioned into the Independent State of Croatia. It was really independent in name only since, from the very beginning, it was nothing more than a Nazi vassal state with a handpicked dictator—Ante Pavelic—at the helm.

At any rate, from this point forward, the Axis nations found themselves in control of the entire Balkan Peninsula. Needless to say, life under the fascists was terrible. It has been said that in the Yugoslavian region alone, about a million people were killed. Due to Adolf Hitler's determination to commit genocide against the Jewish people, a large majority of these deaths were Jews. Tragically enough, it is said that as much as 80 percent of the Jewish population of the Balkans was wiped out.

But the fascists were not the only ones killing people. Toward the end of the war, resistance fighters gained more ground, and they began to engage in reprisals of their own, killing so-called collaborators wholesale. One of the most infamous of these Balkan resistance fighters was Josip Broz Tito, better known simply as Tito. He would become the future strongman of Yugoslavia.

Without getting too terribly bogged down in all the details of the rest of the war, as the conflict progressed, the Allied powers of the United States, Britain, and the Soviet Union were able to systematically dismantle the Axis. First, they took down Italy, then Germany, and—with a struggle—finally Japan.

However, even before the war was over, the Allies were already making big plans for the Balkans. At the Yalta Conference in February of 1945, the three main Allied leaders—US President Franklin Roosevelt, British Prime Minister Winston Churchill, and Soviet Premier Joseph Stalin—hammered out their vision of what a post-war Balkan Peninsula would look like. As the Great Powers of Europe had done in the past, these three world leaders decided to divide the Balkans between themselves into the so-called "spheres of influence."

It was determined that Greece would be under the British and American jurisdiction, while Bulgaria and Romania would be a part of the Soviet sphere of influence. Yugoslavia, in the meantime, would be dismembered once again into various lands that were divided between the Western and Eastern Blocs.

In the Soviet-controlled regions, communism was, of course, a given, although the illusion of elections still took place. Despite the façade of a choice, opponents of communism were regularly jailed, intimidated, or even murdered. Needless to say, if a country holds elections and regularly has political opponents thrown in jail or executed, this is typically not a good sign that free elections are being held. The persecution of political opponents is generally not too good for any hope of having a real democracy.

In the beginning, much of this bullying at the ballot box was probably not even necessary. Many in the Balkans initially had a favorable view of communism. After all, the communists promised to uplift the poor and bring equality. It sounded good in practice to many of the impoverished Balkan masses.

But when the promise of a better life never materialized and oppression and restrictions increased, it became clear to the people that communism was a raw deal. Nevertheless, faced with circumstances outside of their control, the people of the Balkans had once again found themselves on the front lines. The Cold War had just begun.

Chapter 8 – The Cold War and Its Aftermath

"I am the leader of one country which has two alphabets, three languages, four religions, five nationalities, six republics, surrounded by seven neighbors, a country in which live eight ethnic minorities."

-Josip Broz Tito

The Balkans fell like a house of cards as the Soviet Union advanced. The Soviets first penetrated Romania in 1944, chasing after the joint German and Romanian troops. Shortly afterward, the fascist friendly king of Romania, King Mihai (or Michael) I, stepped down, and the Romanians switched sides and joined the Soviets. One after the other, other Balkan states followed suit.

Many of these Balkan regions being liberated by the Soviets identified with Russian history, especially the shared history of the Orthodox Church. The people of the Balkans had long viewed Russia as their "big Orthodox brother." Little did they know that under the Soviet system, the Orthodox Church was being repressed. This was definitely not the same Russia that had helped free the Balkan peoples from Ottoman domination.

But nevertheless, the Balkan people's natural sympathy toward Russia remained, which would help to smooth over much of the Soviet Union's communist takeover of the Balkans. Homegrown communist leaders had wide levels of support. The support of some local communists was meager, but the support of others, such as Yugoslavia's Josip Broz, better known as Tito, was very strong.

But in the aftermath of the war, when it came to whether or not a communist government would remain in place, how popular the local despot was often had little to do with it. As long as that section of the Balkans was under the Soviet Union's sphere of influence, the Soviets were bound and determined to make sure that particular part of the Balkans maintained a communist regime.

This was abundantly clear, for example, in Romania, where communism—especially Soviet-style communism—was not popular at the time. Unlike other Balkan nations, Romania, for the most part, did not have a very favorable view of the Russians. The Romanians had a Catholic background, so they were traditionally closer to the west than the Russian east, and needless to say, the outbreak of recent hostilities between the two certainly did not help matters.

Due to this natural disenchantment with Soviet influence, turning Romania into a communist nation took considerably more work on the part of the Soviets. The Soviets backed a sham election in 1946, in which the communists somehow magically received two-thirds of the total vote. This was quite a feat since most of the country was against communism.

Most Romanians probably did not like the idea of handing over the regions of Bukovina and Bessarabia to the Soviets either. However, their government was made to sign the Paris Treaty, which dealt out reparations and other concessions from World War II, on February 10th, 1947, and these territories suddenly belonged to the Soviet Union. If it were any consolation, the Romanians were at least handed back Transylvania, which they had lost during the war. The Romanian king stepped down that very year and exiled himself to

Switzerland. Shortly thereafter, the Romanian People's Republic was declared.

Bulgaria, for its part, attempted to play both sides and failed. Although Bulgaria initially sided with the Axis during the war, as soon as it seemed that Germany was going to lose, Bulgaria still attempted to come out on the winning side. In 1944, they suddenly declared themselves to be neutral, and when the Soviets were closing in, they even took the extra step of declaring war on the Germans.

But such token lip service was not going to be enough. When local communist agitators—the few that were there—rose up against the Bulgarian government, the Russians took this as their pretext to invade and help the local agitators topple the Bulgarian government. Once in power, these Soviet-backed Bulgarian communists began to terrorize any potential political rivals. This caused any goodwill that the average Bulgarian may have had for them to quickly disappear.

But since the communists were backed by their Soviet taskmasters, there was very little that the Bulgarians could do to dislodge them or the system of government that had been foisted upon them. In November of 1945, both the British and the Americans put forth criticism of the electoral process in Bulgaria, claiming that the whole thing was automatically tilted toward the communists, bolstering criticism of the system, which was already present in Bulgaria. Nevertheless, the communist machine in Bulgaria would continue to move forward.

Serbia and Hungary were also brought into the Soviet orbit. Albania announced its communist "People's Republic" in January of 1946, while the newly christened Federal People's Republic of Yugoslavia was ratifying its constitution. Yugoslavia's Tito then pursued his two main objectives—nationalizing all industries in Yugoslavia and liquidating any and all opposition to his regime.

The following year, 1947, Yugoslavia was denied repatriation of Trieste by the Treaty of Paris while retaining almost all of Istria. Perhaps the Western powers were wary of Tito's closeness to the

Soviets. That same year, British Prime Minister Winston Churchill famously spoke of the "Iron Curtain" that had descended upon Europe. Nevertheless, the Tito regime marched forward, instituting his so-called "five-year plan" in which major industrial reforms were implemented.

Soviet leader Joseph Stalin supported these communist regimes not just for the furtherance of communism but also because he felt it necessary to create loyal buffer states all along Russia's western flank. In light of the attitude of Russian leaders in the 2020s—notably Vladimir Putin's attempts to create a buffer state out of Ukraine—it seems that this is still a desirable policy for the Russian leadership.

Russia's build-up of loyal nations in the East prompted the Western powers to counteract it by establishing NATO (the North Atlantic Treaty Organization), which would serve as a bulwark to counteract the Eastern communist bloc. Greece and Turkey ended up joining NATO in 1952, hemming the Soviets in even further. With these two ideologically opposed camps staring each other down in Europe, it often seemed that armed conflict would be inevitable.

It could be argued that the mutually assured destruction of nuclear war may have been the only thing to have prevented such a conflict from breaking out. The Soviet Union developed nuclear weapons shortly after the United States, and it was soon equal to its rival superpower. Once that happened, direct conflict between the US and the USSR was typically deemed a suicidal course of action by either party since any conventional conflict would most likely turn into a nuclear one. It would be rather difficult for either side to claim much of a victory while having to claw their way out from a pile of radioactive rubble.

So, despite all the saber-rattling of the Cold War, cooler, calmer heads prevailed. Still, the Western world grew increasingly wary of the Eastern Bloc, of which most of the Balkans were a part—and these nations were increasingly aligned against this build-up.

While the bombed-out nations of post-war Western Europe were being showered with US dollars through the Marshall Plan, the Balkans were largely dependent upon the Soviet Union for development and security. Tito stood out among Balkan leaders due to his strident communist outlook and strongarm tactics. He often used force to implement his will on Yugoslavia, and his tactics were embraced by none other than Soviet Premier Joseph Stalin.

Stalin determined that Belgrade would become the capital city of Yugoslavia. And it was here that he inserted the headquarters for Cominform—the nerve center of communist propaganda for the Eastern Bloc. Cominform would remain in place until about a year after the formation of the Warsaw Pact in 1955. The Warsaw Pact bound the entire Eastern Bloc together, and it would be just as binding and impactful for the Balkans as well.

However, problems would soon erupt between Yugoslavia and Soviet Russia when Tito apparently became a little too big for his britches. Tito strongly condemned the United States and the inroads of capitalist ideology in Western Europe, which gained a lot of attention. Suddenly, it seemed that Tito was almost trying to outdo Stalin due to his harsh rhetoric. Even more alarming to Moscow was Tito's penchant for engaging in unilateral foreign policy decisions that had the potential for much larger ramifications without consulting the Soviet government first.

This was an intolerable situation for the Soviet high command. Joseph Stalin did not desire to be overshadowed by a Balkan dictator, and he soon sought to put Tito back in his place. Tito wished to create a confederation of Balkan states, and he engaged in several agreements with fellow Balkan countries, such as Bulgaria, Romania, and Albania, with whom he established a separate Balkan Communist Customs Union.

Tito desired to expand this customs union to Greece, which at that time had not yet made its mind up on whether to embrace communism. In 1948, Tito inserted himself in the ongoing Greek

Civil War, actually posting Yugoslavian troops in nearby Albania. Once again, Tito had done something without consulting Stalin first. Along with being insulted at Tito's lack of respect, Stalin had the very real fear that Tito's "adventurism" could bring down the wrath of the West and lead to a third world war, which would be, even Stalin's mind, an unnecessary world war.

If World War III was going to erupt, Stalin wanted to be the cause of it. He wouldn't want to get involved by reacting to events sparked by that upstart Tito. Infuriated, Stalin told Tito to take no action unless he was given authority from him to do so. Furthermore, he demanded that any idea of a Balkan federation be nixed unless full Soviet oversight could be established.

To Stalin's amazement, Tito stood his ground. No matter how much Stalin fumed and raged, Tito obstinately declined to listen to his entreaties. This led to Stalin bringing forth an official Cominform conference in Bucharest in June of 1948, in which Tito was openly condemned. The conference actually called for Yugoslavia to immediately change course or to have the Tito administration replaced.

However, this Balkan leader was not going to be cowed by the Soviets, and Tito answered the call to have him removed by condemning the Soviet Union itself. Stalin was no doubt shocked by Tito's audacity, but his options were limited. He could either send in troops and waste time, manpower, and resources occupying a fellow communist country, or he could see to it that the rest of the Eastern Bloc ostracized Tito and Yugoslavia as unwelcome pariahs. He chose the latter.

Cominform cut all ties with Yugoslavia, and all members who even had a hint of a relationship with Tito were dismissed. Albania, where Tito wanted to place troops to help Greek communists, immediately shunned the Yugoslavians. Other Balkan countries bordering Yugoslavia became hostile enough that border skirmishes erupted. Yugoslavia itself became an isolated fortress, with literal fortifications put up all along its border passes. There was even talk in Soviet circles of engineering the breakup of Yugoslavia (several decades before it actually happened) and creating more Soviet-friendly mini-Balkan republics from the ashes.

Yet, despite all of this pressure from the outside world to have Tito's regime collapse, he continued to hang on. Not only that, he shocked the communist world by actually reaching out to Western powers, such as the United States and Britain. The West soon realized that the disunity of communism in the Balkans was to their advantage, and they jumped at the chance to drive a wedge between the communists. In 1950, when Yugoslavia was suffering crop failure, it was the Americans who swooped in with robust economic aid. They also openly supplied military aid to the Balkan state.

Such moves were, no doubt, bold on the part of the United States, and the Americans had to walk a tightrope unless they inadvertently provoked a Soviet response. But short of establishing American military bases and putting troops on the ground, America made it clear that they wanted to prop up Tito's defiant regime as a permanent thorn in the Soviet Union's side. Along with his newfound American support, Tito also ended up embracing the emerging Greek government, and he signed a pact with both Greece and Turkey in 1953. This then grew into a full-blown mutual defense treaty, which came about in 1954.

Despite its communist roots, Yugoslavia became a vital Western ally. Tito stood tall as an example of how a communist nation could remain independent from Soviet control. As such, he helped to kick off what would become known as the Non-Aligned Movement. The Non-Aligned Movement was established in 1961 as a coalition of countries that found themselves neither in the Eastern or Western camps. Balkan countries like Tito's also decided to dispense with some of the classic practices of Marxism, such as collectivized crop cultivation, in favor of more traditional private farms, which had long been a part of Balkan history. In essence, if it was not working for the

Balkan way of life, those who followed Tito and Yugoslavia's example were encouraged to jettison the practice.

Stalin had perished in 1953, and he was replaced by Nikita Khrushchev, who denounced Stalin's actions. Throughout much of the 1960s, the Soviets would attempt to mend their broken relations with the Balkans.

More importantly, Khrushchev seemed to bolster the Non-Aligned Movement in the Balkans by stating that communist nations did not have to "blindly follow" every single aspect of the Soviet model of communism. This perhaps had some unintended consequences, however. Rather than following the Soviet model, the Balkan state of Albania began to follow the Chinese model!

China officially became communist in 1949, and it had slowly been making inroads as a leading communist nation. In the 1960s, Albanian leader Enver Hoxha encouraged relations between his state and China. Hoxha actually began to implement reforms in the Balkans that were similar to Chinese leader Mao Zedong's Cultural Revolution.

He bombarded his people with steady propaganda and even mobilized "minders," similar to China's infamous Red Guards, to make sure that citizens did not step out of line with the groupthink of the communist regime. Hoxha wanted to have his citizens mind their manners at home while he expressed outrage over developments abroad. Angered by the Soviet intervention in Czechoslovakia in 1968, Albania actually went as far as to officially renounce its position in the Warsaw Pact.

Unlike Czechoslovakia and Hungary, which were vulnerable to direct Soviet intervention (Albania had the non-aligned country of Yugoslavia as a buffer state), there was little the Soviets could do but voice their disdain. China, in the meantime, as a growing communist power, was quite pleased to have made inroads in the Balkans and supplied generous aid to the Albanians.

Demonstrating the limits of political power based upon the cult of leadership, after Mao Zedong passed away in 1976, Albanian ties to China became virtually nonexistent. And when Albanian's rival Tito paid China a visit in 1977, the Albanian government became downright hostile. The situation became so tense that China actually suspended all Albanian aid in 1978, which led to severe economic disruptions in this Balkan country. Albania continued to decline throughout the 1980s until communism finally collapsed outright.

The Balkan state of Romania had a totally different experience. The Romanians were considered largely loyal to the Soviets throughout much of the Cold War, yet they, too, suffered a severe decline by the 1980s. Romania's communist regime would become yet another failed communist state by the end of the Cold War, and the regime would be forcefully removed by its own people in 1989.

After Romanian dictator Nicolae Ceausescu was unable to rein in protests against his regime, a revolt erupted that ended in the execution of both Nicolae and his wife, Elena. Romania had perhaps the most dramatic regime change in the Balkans, but in short order, all forms of communism would soon come to an end in the Balkans.

After the collapse of communism in the Balkans, the lines of many Balkan countries were redrawn. The breakup of Yugoslavia, of course, was the most drastic. Yugoslavia ultimately split apart into the following countries: Serbia, Croatia, Slovenia, Montenegro, Bosnia and Herzegovina, and Macedonia. The tensions between different ethnicities and religions in these regions, which had been fused together under communism, would boil to the surface in the worst way in the late 1990s.

Bosnia would explode into violence when Bosnian Serbs and Bosnian Croatians began to battle one another. Serbian President Slobodan Milosevic fanned these flames by throwing his weight behind the Bosnian Serbs. This led to terrible bloodshed, as the two groups fought each other from 1992 to 1995. The Serbs, in particular, would be accused of "ethnic cleansing" in what was allegedly their push to create a Serbian state. This violence led to the United States and NATO becoming involved.

Russia was a bit too preoccupied with the ongoing restructuring of its post-Soviet world to take an active role in all of this. Russian President Boris Yeltsin did, however, occasionally issue warnings to the West not to meddle with the affairs of Russia's "Slavic brothers."

In all, it is estimated that approximately 100,000 Bosnians perished in this conflict, and millions more were reduced to refugee status since they were driven from their ancestral lands. As the violence threatened to spiral out of control, NATO intervened, launching Operation Deliberate Force.

The name of this military operation might sound a little nonsensical. After all, what military operation does not use deliberate force? But despite the oddity of its title, the operation did indeed achieve its objectives. The main fighting ended with the signing of the Dayton Peace Accords on December 14th, 1995, yet this was not the end of the conflict.

Ethnic Albanians began to struggle against partisans of the Kosovo Liberation Army in the region of Kosovo. At this time, Kosovo was a province of Serbia. Slobodan Milosevic, of course, backed the Serbs once again, this time against the Albanian Kosovars, who had a large Muslim population. The fighting soon became a horrendous mix of ethnic and religious hostilities.

Lest the violence spill out to the rest of the Balkans, NATO made the decision to bomb the Serbian forces. The result of this bombing campaign, along with other international pressures, was a Serbian defeat and the establishment of the independent state of Kosovo. It also forced Slobodan Milosevic from power. He was hauled off to imprisonment in The Hague, where he died from a heart attack in 2006.

Not everyone was happy with Kosovo's declaration of independence. Greece, for one, still does not recognize Kosovo's

NATO-given status. Romania and Bulgaria actually joined NATO in 2003. They then followed up this feat by gaining entrance into the European Union in 2007. Slovenia had already earned this privilege in 2004.

Becoming members of both of these international organizations is appealing to many Balkan states, but doing so or even suggesting a desire to do so could bring forth many unforeseen consequences.

Ukraine is generally not considered a part of the Balkans, with the possible exception of Crimea. But nevertheless, this nation serves as a great example of the Pandora's box that can be opened in light of the Ukraine/Russia tensions, which erupted into full-blown war in 2022. Ever since the end of the Cold War, many parts of the Balkans have faced the same kinds of pressures of feeling inevitably torn between the East and the West.

Conclusion: Memories of a Common History in Bulk

The Balkans have always been a complicated place. As the crossroads of southeastern Europe, they have seen several empires rise and fall. Several different tribes of people have passed through these lands. And wars have been fought over just about every religion and ideology under the sun. Balkan history is so complex that it is often hard to put it all into words.

It is difficult to summarize how the history of a country such as Greece, which is most known for its role in the spread of Hellenism and its role in classical antiquity, relates to the Balkan states of Albania and Kosovo. It is also hard to consider the diverging fates of Catholic Romania and staunchly Orthodox Bulgaria, but all of these diverging histories are part of the Balkans.

In the Balkans, you get a little bit of everything. And the history of its residents is often perceived as being history in bulk, one that is intertwined with each nation. But as much as we try to lump the Balkans together, the incredibly complex history of this region compels us to take a closer look. Only in doing so are we able to see a more detailed picture of the many complex problems, peoples, and developments that have taken place in the geopolitical tract of land commonly known as the Balkans.

Here's another book by Captivating History
that you might like

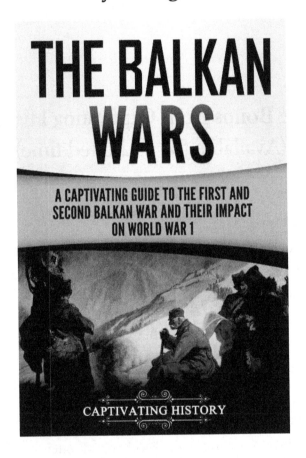

Free Bonus from Captivating History
(Available for a Limited time)

Hi History Lovers!

Now you have a chance to join our exclusive history list so you can get your first history ebook for free as well as discounts and a potential to get more history books for free! Simply visit the link below to join.

Captivatinghistory.com/ebook

Also, make sure to follow us on Facebook, Twitter and Youtube by searching for Captivating History.

Appendix A: Further Reading and Reference

Cross & Crescent in the Balkans: The Ottoman Conquest of South Eastern Europe. David Nicolle. 2010.

Ghost Empire: A Journey to the Legendary Constantinople. Richard Fidler. 2017.

The Ottoman Empire: 1326-1699. Stephen Turnbull. 2003.

The Balkans: From Constantinople to Communism. Dennis P. Hupchick. 2002.

Made in United States
North Haven, CT
10 August 2023

40181380R00055